THE
MONUMENTAL
CEMETERIES
OF PREHISTORIC EUROPE

MAGDALENA S. MIDGLEY

TEMPUS

In loving memory of my father-in-law
John Midgley (1911-2000)

First published 2005

Tempus Publishing Ltd
The Mill, Brimscombe Port
Stroud, Gloucestershire GL5 2QG
www.tempus-publishing.com

British Library Cataloguing in Publication Data.
A catalogue record for this book is available from the British Library.

ISBN 0 7524 2567 6

Typesetting and design by Liz Rudderham
Origination by Tempus Publishing.
Printed and bound in Great Britain.

CONTENTS

LIST OF ILLUSTRATIONS

Colour Plates

ACKNOWLEDGEMENTS

Over the years many colleagues, deliberately or unwittingly, helped to shape my ideas on the European Neolithic. In that sense I am indebted to too many individuals to name them all but I hope that my general acknowledgement will be appreciated as a proper recognition of the contribution they have made to my intellectual and academic progress. There are, however, those who have made a more direct impact on the writing and the preparation of this book and I should like to offer specific thanks to the following: Peter Bogucki, Clive Bonsall, Serge Cassen, Lyn Collins, Pascal Duhamel, Frédéric Lontcho, Arkadiusz Marciniak, Ian Morrison, Marek Nowak, Jean-Pierre Pautreau, Ivan Pavlů, Professor V. Podborský, Chris Scarre and Miroslav Šmíd.

Two individuals deserve particular acknowledgement: Dr Catriona Pickard assisted with many of the tasks involved in preparing this book, including the illustrations. My husband Stephen was ever ready with his red pen to improve my English, to suggest better phrases and move the commas and semicolons to where they ought to be. I thank them both heartily.

The book was written during the sabbatical period kindly agreed by the University of Edinburgh; part of chapter 2 has previously been published in *Archeologické rozhledy* 54 (Midgley 2002). I also acknowledge with thanks the financial assistance from the University of Edinburgh Development Trust Research Fund. The excavations at Escolives-Sainte-Camille in Burgundy received financial support from the British Academy, the Carnegie Trust and the Munro Trust.

PREFACE

For the past century-and-a-half the Neolithic period has held a very special place in the prehistory of north-west Europe. It was, of course, a time of dramatic changes: the initial late nineteenth-century definitions clearly revolved around new technologies such as polished stone axes, and new economies in the form of domesticated plants and animals, emphasising very strongly the significance of economic parameters which, for many scholars, retain their attraction to this day.

However, even more profound changes were taking place outwith the Neolithic economic sphere. Beyond the creation of fields, pastures and villages, the men and women were developing new ways of looking at the world in which they lived: these included views about themselves, their neighbours both near and far, new sets of religious ideas and social interactions, as well as different ways of expressing concerns about individuals and communities. Indeed, the most enduring and dramatic images of the period from the sixth to the fourth millennia BC are those which express that vital bond between the communities of the living and the dead.

We are all familiar, be it from specialist or popular literature, as well as through television images, with the spiritual world of our ancestors that is so well encapsulated in the different forms of megalith found in profusion from the Atlantic coastline in the west to the Baltic shores in the north. However, some communities found equally ostentatious ways of dealing with their dead which put less emphasis on the use of stone as the construction medium and, consequently, have left less visible traces in the landscape. This book deals with one such form of burial – the so-called earthen long barrows – which in some areas of north-west Europe form veritable cemeteries.

My personal interest in these monuments goes back to the days of my first ever piece of research for an undergraduate dissertation. There I attempted to explore some of the issues raised by these monuments in my native Poland, which subsequently led to a geographically wider consideration of this topic in northern Europe. Since then I have explored other aspects of the Neolithic in northern Europe, but that fascination with the long barrows has never quite ebbed away. Indeed, it was the excitement of the research into this type of monument in France that brought me back to this subject. The opportunity to become involved in the excavation of one of these cemeteries – at Escolives-Sainte-Camille in Burgundy – was too tempting to ignore.

Virtually unknown until the early 1980s, there are now dozens of monumental long barrow cemeteries identified through aerial photography in the northern and central part of France, and doubtless many more will come to light in the next decade. Quite appropriately, these sites have been exciting French Neolithic researchers, although there is by no means uniform agreement as to their status in relation to that classic French Neolithic burial form – the megalithic tomb. However, it is only fair to say that in other areas little research has taken place since my initial study; one is eagerly awaiting some new discoveries across north-western Germany – surely an entirely artificial gap between the region of Kujavia in central Poland and the Paris Basin.

In this book, therefore, I incorporate the evidence from the French long barrow cemeteries into the framework of my own understanding of the significance of the long barrow monumental architecture across north-western Europe. Since my earlier research, some of our perceptions of Neolithic society have undergone profound changes for the better and my own ideas have also altered: I have abandoned some views, while others have become even more entrenched!

The reader should therefore be aware that this is not a new, in-depth study of the long barrow phenomenon – this sort of task I leave appropriately to some future enterprising PhD student who wishes to cut their teeth on the various hurdles presented by such research. Instead I offer, in what I hope is a popular form to appeal to the student as well as the general interested reader, a reappraisal of some of the major issues revolving around the significance of the monumental cemeteries.

In raising these cemeteries, the communities of the middle of the fifth millennium BC embarked upon a remarkable transformation of the natural environment by creating permanent abodes for their dead. These, as well as the cultural and ideological setting within which they were created, cannot be understood in a vacuum. Hence the departure point for our discussion is, inevitably, the cultural and social background of the preceding period – the time when the late hunter-gatherers and early farmers were neighbours, in the wider sense of the term, in many areas of north-west Europe (chapter 1). It was their interaction which, over a period of at least a millennium, created the conditions for the emergence in north-west Europe of distinctly local farming groups (chapter 2). Both the late Mesolithic hunter-gatherers and the Danubian farmers articulated their attitude to the dead through clear if very different forms of burial rituals and practices (chapter 3). As I try to explain, both traditions were dynamic – with rituals changing in accordance with the needs of the living communities – and both ultimately contributed to the emergence of a wholly new set of attitudes towards the dead.

The long barrow cemeteries themselves can be viewed from a variety of angles: the actual appearance of the monuments was important not only in terms of the visual and cultural impact they created within the landscape and their relationship with both past and contemporary settlement patterns (chapter 4), but also in terms of the actual burial ritual which imaginatively combined features typical of the previous hunter-gatherer and Danubian burial practices (chapter 5).

It is one thing, however, to perceive the archaeological record, but quite another matter to offer a convincing and meaningful interpretation. The ultimate significance of the long barrow cemeteries, and of their connections to the past as well as projections into the future (chapter 6), is thus seen from the subjective stance of a researcher with a very personal vision of the Neolithic way of life and death.

CHAPTER ONE

EUROPE BEFORE
THE TIME
OF THE LONG BARROWS

THE LATE MESOLITHIC HUNTER–GATHERERS

The late Mesolithic communities are important to our investigation for several reasons. First of all, they are heirs to the immensely rich social and cultural traditions developed from the ninth millennium BC onwards, traditions which not only persisted but played an important role in the shaping of the future European cultural mosaic. Secondly, the diversity of the late Mesolithic communities is a testimony to the dynamic nature of the hunter-gatherer world: we perceive them as economically and technologically resourceful, engaged in elaborate social processes leading to the enhancement of the individual's social standing, and possessing a clear vision of their place within the natural and cultural world. Finally, and most importantly, they did not live in isolation but were active participants in a social and economic world that included people with a vastly different lifestyle – the Neolithic farmers – and thus they contributed to the creation of the subsequent cultural make-up of north-west Europe.

Throughout the vast area from where the Loire discharges its waters into the Atlantic in the west, to the Baltic and Scania in the north, different late Mesolithic entities have been identified which, while sharing a number of characteristics, differ sufficiently from one another to merit recognition as individual cultural groups (1).

Thus, along the French Atlantic coastline, the Mesolithic specialists distinguish the so-called Retzian, named after the area of Retz and centred around the Loire estuary, and the Téviecian, named after the Téviec shell-midden, and known along the south Breton littoral as well as further inland (Marchand 1999, 2000). The Paris Basin and areas further to the north and east are home to the so-called Tardenosian (Thévenin 1999) but, once we move over to the

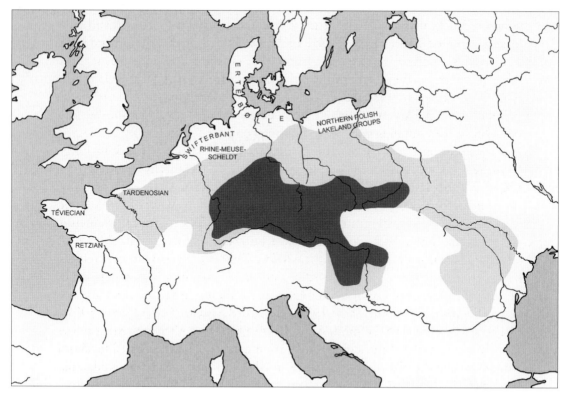

1 Distribution of the Danubian *Linearbandkeramik* culture (dark – oldest; pale – maximum extent) and major late Mesolithic groups in north-west Europe. *Lüning 1988; Midgley 1992; Marchand 1999; Raemaekers 1999*

Low Countries, the extension of this complex is known under the name Rhine-Meuse-Scheldt culture and reaches over to the area of Trèves and Eifel in north-west Germany (Street *et al.* 2003).

There are further complexities: in the lowlands between the Scheldt and the lower Elbe – encompassing parts of the Netherlands and Lower Saxony – the Swifterbant culture has recently been defined (Raemaekers 1999). It is seen as a counterpart, even if a more enterprising one, to the so-called Ertebølle culture named after one of the large shell-middens on the Limfjord in north Jutland. The latter occupied a substantial part of northern Europe: we encounter it in Schleswig-Holstein, Mecklenburg and as far east as the Polish Baltic coast. Further late Mesolithic groups, for some of which Ertebølle affinities have been claimed, are present in the area of northern and central Poland (Ilkiewicz 1989).

Geographically, the area of north-west Europe offers a complex mosaic of landscape relief, soils and water networks which, together with the optimal thermal conditions of the Atlantic period, provided a diversity of natural environments. The mixed oak forests dominant over lowland and upland landscapes supported rich mammalian populations with red and roe deer, auroch and wild boar among the larger species, while coastlines as well as estuaries, inland lakes and rivers supported a wide variety of waterfowl, bird, fish and shell species. Thus many areas offered environments with a wide range of natural resources. The abundance and regional diversity of local environments in north-west Europe were particularly suitable for settlement and exploitation by late Mesolithic communities with wide-ranging economic strategies.

Certain areas may well have been suitable for permanent, or at least long-term, seasonal occupation. This seems to be most dramatically evidenced on the large shell-middens of the Scandinavian and Atlantic coasts (*køkkenmødding* in Danish and *amas coquillier* in French).★ Although the majority of the Atlantic shell-middens lie directly on the coast – indeed the famous Téviec midden is today an off-shore island – originally these sites were further inland as the local sea level was at least 20m lower than today. This is important to our under-standing of the nature of these sites since their function was much more eclectic, involving the use of numerous inland resources as much as making use of marine habitats (Péquart *et al.* 1937; Péquart M. and S.J. 1954; Kayser 1991). Shell-middens are artificial mounds of marine shells and other settlement refuse that have accumulated through a long period of use of specific coastal localities (some of the Danish middens were used over one-and-a-half millennia; Andersen S.H. 2000b). Their significance lies not only in the excellent preser-vation of organic materials – especially valuable in the context of the acid soils – but also in the information they provide on subsistence, seasonality and stratigraphy, so lacking from contemporary open-air sites.

Evidence from the living floors is difficult to interpret, but possible house structures are suggested by stake-hole patterns on the Danish sites or by cavities dug into the rock on Breton sites (Beg-en-Dorchen). Stone-built circular hearths up to 1.5m in diameter and cooking pits are common in both regions. Areas immediately outside the shell-middens investigated in Denmark suggest that occupation was not limited to the midden itself, but extended well beyond (Andersen S.H. 1993; Andersen S.H. and Johansen 1987).

Shell-middens, however, are only one among many types of settlement location along the coast and many other sites, which do not have shell layers, are part of the contemporary settlement pattern. Indeed, the Danish Braband and Dyrholmen sites fall into this category and many 'open-air' coastal sites have been identified elsewhere: Dąbki on the Polish Baltic coast, the numerous late Mesolithic sites on the island of Rügen, Wangels in East Holstein, and a whole range of open-air sites along the Atlantic littoral, such as Saint-Gildas or

---

★The Mesolithic shell-middens have a long history of research, dating in both areas well into the nineteenth century: in 1848 the first Danish *køkkenmødding* commission was set up with the purpose of systematically investigating the shell-middens in an interdisciplinary context and its work was quickly disseminated in European scientific circles; the Breton investigations were not so strictly regulated, but the 1880s work of Du Chatellier and his associates led to the earliest excavations of the key Breton sites at Téviec and Beg-en-Dorchen.

la Giladière near the Loire estuary (Ilkiewicz 1989; Gramsch 1973; Hartz 1998; Marchand 1999, 2000).

Although late Mesolithic inland sites have been known for a long time, for example at Ringkloster in Denmark and Boberg or Dümmer in north Germany, many more have been discovered recently in all regions of north-west Europe. Thus, investigations in the lake districts of north-east Poland have brought to light many sites in lacustrian environments: the late Mesolithic site at Dudka in Masuria is typical of such sites, and its location has been described as a paradise for hunting and fishing (Gumiński 1998). The fresh and brackish water creek systems at Swifterbant and the river dunes at Hazendonk in the Netherlands supported late Mesolithic settlements; indeed the conditions there seem to have been conducive to early experiments with agricultural economy (Raemaekers 1999). Recent work in the Somme valley area has identified many sites on the edges of plateaux, the most important being the Mesolithic cemetery and settlement at Petit-Marais, La Chaussée-Tirancourt (Ducrocq 1999), and research in the Paris Basin has also revealed numerous late Mesolithic sites with settlement and burial evidence, notably at Auneau (Verjux 1999a).

Due to their excellent preservation of organic materials, the shell-middens demonstrate a broad-spectrum cuisine enjoyed by the late hunter-gatherers. Of course marine shells were important: oysters (*Ostrea sp.*), cockles (*Cerastoderma edulis*), mussels (*Mytilus edulis*), limpets (*Patella vulgata*) and periwinkles (*Littorina littorea*) were collected seasonally, although they may have been a source of important minerals such as zinc, iodine and salts rather than just a food 'stop-gap' for the lean season (Andersen S.H. 2000, 380). However, bone remains of marine as well as terrestrial animals suggest that both types of food were consumed on the shell-middens.

Marine species are well represented: shark, skate, bream and whale (the latter possibly beached) were caught along the Atlantic coast, while seals, flatfish, cod and eel were consumed in Denmark. A survey of Danish fish bones from the Mesolithic coastal settlements includes 41 species. (Bødker Enghoff 1995, 67, Table 1). In both areas marine as well as migrating birds were caught. Anadromous fish such as salmon, sea trout, sturgeon or grey mullet were partic-ularly important in estuarine localities, while on lacustrian and riverine sites freshwater fish such as pike, perch, bream and carp were the most commonly caught species.

Terrestrial animals were important to the Mesolithic diet everywhere. Inland stations, as well as coastal sites – and these include the shell-middens – indicate that large ungulates (red and roe deer), auroch and wild boar were hunted for food, although their contribution in terms of meat varies from one locality to the next. Indeed, results of recent palaeodietary studies have even been inter-preted as indicative of taboos influencing the types of food consumed by indi-viduals (Schulting and Richards 2001; Schulting 2003). As we shall see later, these large mammals were also important in the context of rituals practised by the hunter-gatherers. Smaller animals, such as fox, beaver, pine marten, wildcat and wolf to name but a few, are regularly present in the late Mesolithic bone assemblages across the entire area of north-west Europe. It is generally assumed that they were hunted for their pelts, but one wonders to what extent this view is influenced by modern ethics. Indeed, the presence of such species as buzzard, kestrel, swan, starling and seagull – species not considered consumable today – indicates a very eclectic regime.

Less can be said about the late Mesolithic plant foods. The ubiquitous hazelnut was undoubtedly important, but the rest is largely conjectural because there is little refuse from plant foods, and what was not consumed quickly rotted away. Wild fruits have occasionally been found preserved on Mesolithic sites: pears at Téviec, raspberries at Muldbjerg, crab apple, hawthorn, rose-hip and blackberry are reported from the Swifterbant sites. However, many plant remains, such as edible forest fungi and various tubers, are not likely to have survived and yet they were undoubtedly gathered – as they are to this day – in the forests across the North European Plain. It is reasonable to assume that a great variety of wild plants would have been collected throughout the seasons to provide nourishment and medicines and to add variety to the diet.*

Circumstantial evidence, as well as the ultimate cultivation of cereals in conditions far removed from the original habitats of these plants, argue for profound knowledge and understanding of the plant world among the late Mesolithic communities. One example will suffice: the art of coppicing of willow, birch and hazel is very dramatically documented in Denmark, although it would have been a skill known to and practised by all late Mesolithic communities. Recent investigations in the area of the Storebælt, at the Halsskov Fjord, have brought to light examples of Mesolithic fish traps and weirs. At Margrethes Naes the wreckage of a fishing weir built of hazel and willow stakes, together with a fish trap, is dated to between 5430 and 5390 BC (Myrhøj and Willemoes 1997) and an identical, later, Neolithic fishing weir was located *in situ* at Oleslyst (*2*; Pedersen 1995, 1997). These examples, together with many from other areas, not only inform us about fishing practices which seem to have remained unchanged from the Mesolithic to the Neolithic but, equally significantly, demonstrate that coppicing of such species as hazel and willow was practised from the Mesolithic onwards. Fishing weirs undoubtedly would have been used in suitable locations along the North Sea and Baltic coastlines, and stationary fishing practised along numerous lake shores and rivers across the whole of north-west Europe.

The late Mesolithic hunter-gatherers were skilled craftsmen with a rich toolkit made of flint, stone, bone and antler. While it is precisely the flint industries – in many areas still the principal and, occasionally, the only diagnostic material culture of the late Mesolithic – which serve as a typological foundation for the

*For in-depth discussion see Zvelebil's 1994 review of the evidence for the use of plants in the Mesolithic.

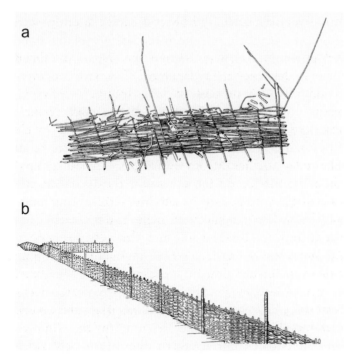

2 Oleslyst, Denmark:
a) fish weir in plan;
b) reconstruction.
Pedersen 1995

definition of different cultural groups outlined above, it is equally important to underline some pan-European characteristics of the late Mesolithic industries.

The previous middle Mesolithic traditions were characterised by the production of hyper-microliths. In contrast, the late Mesolithic industries are based on blade manufacturing technologies – the so-called Montbani style technique designed to produce fine, parallel-sided blades – and geared to the production of a bewildering variety of projectile points among which the trapeze is a dominant form. This technological change took place over large areas of Europe, beginning sometime in the first half of the seventh millennium BC and spreading very quickly. Curiously, this coincides with the appearance, in the south-east of Europe, of the first agricultural communities, although it is difficult to determine whether these two processes were related. Indeed, it seems more appropriate to consider such a technological change to be related to changes in hunting techniques and more efficient use of bows and arrows; the trapezes, developed into transverse arrowheads, provided by far the most lethal hunting tools (Thévenin 1999; Mazurié de Keroualin 2003).

Once again, detailed analysis of different types need not concern us here but it is interesting to note some general trends. First of all, an important difference is the presence of large tools – core and flake flint axes and polished greenstone axes – in the area of the North Sea and the Baltic, components which are largely missing to the west of the Rhine. This may reflect the availability of raw materials suitable for the manufacture of such large tools in the north, with a distinct lack of suitably sized nodules in the west. On the other hand, this assortment of large tools was very important in heavier domestic activities such as woodworking.

The typological development of arrowheads from the trapezoidal forms typical of the second half of the seventh millennium BC towards an ever-increasing range which, from 6000 BC onwards, includes many evolved types, shows an interesting pattern. Asymmetrical trapezes in the west (France, Belgium and westernmost parts of Germany) are retouched on the left, while further to the north and east they are retouched on the right. This forms an important technological boundary, particularly if viewed against the background of the rapid dissemination of the trapeze as a form, between the west and east – its blurring, observed towards the very end of the late Mesolithic, being interpreted as evidence for significant demographic movements in this zone.

Tools made of organic materials – bone, wood or antler – survive only in special conditions: on shell-middens or in waterlogged environments. In spite of the selective distribution of such environments, it is clear that the Mesolithic toolkit included a wide range of tools made of organic materials. Breton shell-middens have yielded antler picks, various bone points and pins, some decorated. T-shaped antler axes seem to have been used everywhere, although the best preserved examples derive from northern Europe in Schleswig-Holstein and southern Scandinavia. Indeed, it is the latter regions which provide the richest evidence for items made of various organic materials (*3*).

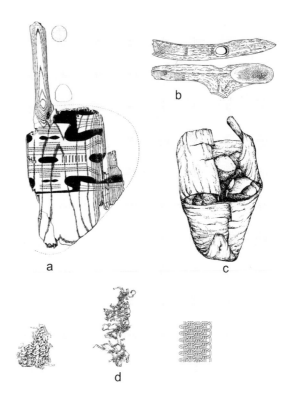

3 Organic artefacts from late Mesolithic contexts: a) ornamental paddle from Tybrind Vig;
b) T-shaped antler axe from Dąbki;
c) bark storage vessel from Friesack;
d) textiles from Tybrind Vig.
Gramsch 1993; Ilkiewicz 1989; Malm 1995

As an example, we may consider the finds from the submerged Ertebølle settlement at Tybrind Vig, off the west coast of Fyn, which offer a profound insight into the richness of the late Mesolithic toolkit. Apart from the remains of fish traps and a range of fishing gear – leisters, spears, harpoons – the most spectacular finds include textiles spun from plant fibres, limewood dugout canoes and ashwood paddles, some of the latter ornamented with rich abstract designs (Malm 1995). Elsewhere wooden spades, bone rings and bone combs have been found; the shell, amber and wild animal teeth jewellery adorning the dead is a testimony to the rich artefact world of the late Mesolithic.

THE DANUBIAN FARMERS

From the middle of the sixth millennium BC the area of central Europe became a theatre of profound socio-cultural developments. A farming way of life – with all the dramatic changes it involved – began to spread from Hungary in the east, to reach the Paris Basin towards 5100 BC. The river Danube by and large provided the southern boundary and to the north, farming communities became established as far as the southern fringes of the North European Plain; enterprising groups occasionally ventured even further, creating small enclaves deep into the hunter-gatherers' territory (*1*).

Evoking the Danube – that important prehistoric highway which joins east and west – Gordon V. Childe (1929) referred to these farming communities as the Danubians. This term has not been in much use recently, since typo-chronological refinements of the process of the spread and consolidation of farming in this vast area have highlighted a multitude of different cultural groupings. However, it will serve us here in its generic sense, as advantageous to our understanding of the broader picture of these early farmers.

Sites with Danubian-style ceramics have been known since the nineteenth century onwards, but serious interest began only with the first substantial excavations of the 1930s: Buttler's project at Köln-Lindenthal (Buttler and Haberey 1936) and Jażdżewski's excavations at Brześć Kujawski (Jażdżewski 1938; Gabałówna 1966). During the 1950s and 1960s Bohumil Soudský directed a research programme at the site of Bylany in Bohemia, which acquired world renown on account of its practical, methodological and theoretical approaches to the investigation of early Neolithic settlements (Soudský 1960, 1966, 1970). At the other end of Europe Modderman, much more modestly but with equally important results, was engaged in rescue excavations on sites in the Dutch Limburg (Modderman 1959, 1970). Then the early 1970s saw two massive but very different projects, both relying on rapid, mechanical stripping of large surfaces endangered by industrial activities. One was on the Aldenhovener Platte near Cologne (Farruggia *et al.* 1973; Kuper *et al.* 1997; Lüning and Stehli 1994) and the other east of Paris, in the Aisne valley (Ilett *et al.* 1982; Ilett and Plateaux 1995). These researches, as well as a host of other smaller scale projects, have now contributed a massive resource base for the study of the Danubian settlement across the whole of its distribution area.

In broad terms the Danubian Neolithic comprises the *Linearbandkeramik* (LBK) culture (named after the linear motifs so typical of the earliest central European ceramics) which begins about 5600/5500 BC in Hungary, reaching the Rhineland by about 5300 BC and the Paris Basin − where it is known under the name of *Rubané Récent* − by about 5200/5100 BC. After an apparently serious crisis (Farruggia 2002), the LBK gives rise to a series of related but geographically discrete groups: from Lengyel in the east, via *Stichbandkeramik* and Rössen to Villeneuve-Saint-Germain in the west. Taking into consideration regional variations, these groups belong principally to the first half of the fifth millennium BC (Jeunesse 1999; Farruggia 2002).

There are two diametrically opposed philosophies accounting for the spread of farming in central Europe − colonisation and local development − each with its own vigorous contingent of supporters (Ammerman 1989; Ammerman and Cavalli-Sforza 1973; Price 2000; Whittle 1996; Zvelebil and Rowley-Conwy 1984; Zvelebil and Zvelebil 1988). Much ink has been spilled rehearsing the arguments for or against each of these interpretations, and in the context of our present discussion these need not be aired out again, but we should note that there are considerable problems in a simple acceptance of either scenario and that some scholars, at least, occupy the middle ground between these two extremes.

Mesolithic sites continue to be elusive in areas of the initial farming settlement, and it is impossible to determine whether they are largely nonexistent in these regions or whether we are simply not able to detect them. The speed with which farming established itself over large areas of central Europe, within a period of about 400 years, speaks vividly in favour of a largely uninhabited landscape available for relatively swift colonisation. Moreover, the arrest of the spread of farming at the boundaries of areas for which we have good evidence of hunter-gatherer presence seems to support this hypothesis. On the other hand, we are painfully ignorant of the demographic and social dynamics for that period of prehistory, with the nineteenth-century colonisation models hardly adequate to explain what Bogucki has aptly termed the 'Neolithic diaspora' (Bogucki 2000). Much faith is currently being put in the area of genetics to help to alleviate some of these problems, but even this may not be sufficient to explain a problematic scenario (Bentley *et al.* 2003).

Perhaps we really need to accept that two processes, not easily distinguishable archaeologically, were taking place. At some time and in certain areas farmers were easily able to move from one locality to the next, and this seems to be the case within the area of the oldest LBK presence: in the areas of the middle and upper Danube, the Neckar, as well as the upper reaches of the Elbe, Oder and Vistula. Outwith this initial concentration of early farmers, ideas as well as peoples moved from one area to the next at different paces and across varying distances.

One characteristic of the LBK communities has been aptly encapsulated in one of Modderman's works, *The Linear Pottery Culture: Diversity in Uniformity* (1988) – that of uniformity of the material world which they inhabited. Of course there are differences – seen as much between individual LBK settlements as between regions – but the similarities are so strong that representative materials can immediately be classed as 'Danubian'. Everywhere, from Slovakia to the Netherlands, the LBK represents a fully developed farming economy with a complement of domesticated animals and cereal crops, household and large-scale industrial activities from pottery making to flint mining and stone extraction for the manufacture of tools, with impressive domestic architecture and clearly articulated rituals relating to the living as well as the dead.

The settlement pattern is one of repetitive occupation of fertile loess soils, with sites frequently strung out like beads along the lower terraces of small river valleys. At the northern and western extremities – for example in Kujavia, Pomerania or in the Paris Basin, where loess soils were not available – localities closely approximating loessic environmental conditions were sought out in preference to all others. The settled areas offered good conditions for the raising of stock and cultivation of cereals. Cattle, pig, sheep and goat are represented on most sites, albeit in varying proportions. It has been assumed in the past that hunting, while important in the west, was of no significance in the east. However, as Pavlů has recently pointed out, large-scale hunting was in some cases an important means of subsistence among the newly established settlers (for example at Nové Dvory, near the famous LBK settlement of Bylany; Pavlů 2000, 274), and indeed its role increased considerably among the late Danubian communities in all regions.

Cereal crops such as emmer (*Triticum dicoccum*), einkorn (*Triticum monococcum*), barley (*Hordeum vulgare* L.) or pea (*Pisum sativum* L.) were grown everywhere, although in the west other plants such as poppy (*Papaver somniferum* L.) and flax (*Linum usitatissimum*) were acquired through contacts with the Mediterranean world. The fields are difficult to identify, but cultivated zones were made available through progressive stripping of tree cover in the vicinity of settlements (Stehli 1989). Evidence from the Dutch Limburg, the Aldenhovener Platte and the Aisne river valley unequivocally supports the idea that settlements were permanently occupied and did not rely on cyclical displacement in order to maintain farming practices.

The LBK settlements (*4*) are among the most singular features across the whole Danubian realm, although the density with which they were built up decreases from east to west. The architecture of the long house, originally misinterpreted at Köln-Lindenthal (Buttler and Haberey 1936), was one of the most enduring elements traversing Europe from Hungary to the Netherlands. In ground plan, the houses reveal themselves as rectangular structures defined

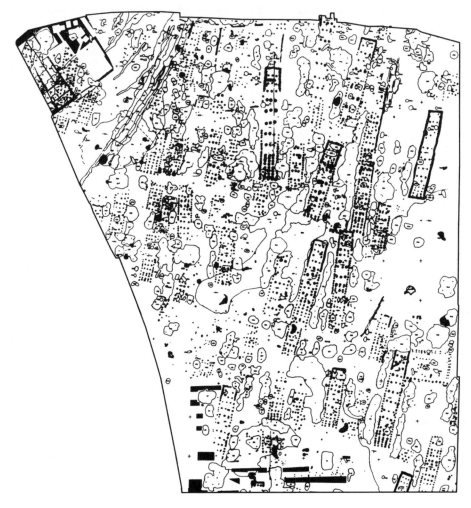

4 Plan of the *Linearbandkeramik* settlement at Bylany (northern part of section A), Bohemia. *With permission of Bylany Archive, Institute of Archaeology, Prague*

by five rows of post holes, with the first and the fifth rows constituting the external walls (*colour plates 1 and 2*). The interior of the house was functionally divided into inner, central and outer parts, although this was not the case with all buildings and accordingly they differed in length. Excavations at Bylany suggest that the very early LBK houses may initially have been rather flimsy (Pavlů 2000, 275) but the construction techniques must have improved very quickly. While the principle of the long house was continued in the later Danubian groups, the architecture changed, with the rectangular shape giving way to a more trapezoidal form and with improved roof-construction techniques, freeing much of the interior from support posts. The layout of the villages also changed, with family houses sometimes closely grouped – as was, for example, typical of the Lengyel groups in Kujavia – or largely on their own as at Bohum-Hiltrop (Brandt 1967).

Apart from its function as a home – in whatever way this would have been understood by the Danubian inhabitants – the long house was clearly a very important social and ideological symbol for the early farmers. This concept will be elaborated later but, for the time being, we may note that the reproduction of this form over a distance of at least 1,500km underlines the significance of architecture for the expression of cultural identity. Bradley has recently suggested that '...the long houses of Neolithic Europe were not only dwellings but monuments in their own right which charted the history of the first farming communities' (Bradley 2001, 55).

It is important to emphasise that, so far, there has not been a single Danubian house found anywhere, since only the barest foundations survive. The reconstruction of activities that took place within and around the houses is based on these ephemeral traces and on the finds preserved in the lateral pits, originally dug to provide the material for the walls. It was only in the 1950s that scholars have agreed that these finds represented the domestic activities associated with individual houses.

Finds from these pits provide the bulk of material on the LBK sites, among which pottery is the most commonly encountered (*colour plate 3*). The Danubians had a wide assortment of ceramics, from large storage vessels to pots for preparation and for the serving of food. The wares were very well made; the decoration initially involves incised curvilinear patterns (frequently spirals) which progressively become more angular and spread over the entire surface. The technique of line incision is later elaborated by short stabs placed at various intervals along the lines – a pattern which recalls musical notation and, not surprisingly, is known as the 'music note' style; geometric bands infilled with multiple impressions are characteristic of the late periods. The ceramics of the later Danubian groups, while continuing some of the LBK decorative principles, display many individual decorative techniques – such as the use of tooth-comb applied in plain or pivotal fashion, or deep stabs. These, together with a wide assortment of motifs, have become diagnostic features for the differentiation of regional groups and countless typo-chronologies have been proposed (Rulf 1997; Zápotocká 1999b; Constantin 1985 provide some examples of such typo-chronologies).

The decorative unity of pottery over large areas expresses not just the functional but the symbolic uniformity of the Danubian world. The patterns are generally regarded as abstract and contrast greatly with the more representative motifs on pottery made by early farmers in the south-east of Europe. While it is true that the degree of abstraction increases the further west we move, this abstraction may well be a result of reinterpretation of natural models. A single example will suffice: a vessel from Bylany with a stylised goat handle and a double spiral either side can be easily interpreted as a stylisation of a bucranium.

While rare, such examples are known in the eastern part of the LBK. Like their houses, pottery decorations also seem to carry references to the mythical ancestral past of the Danubians.

The stone and flint tools made by the Danubians comprise a wide range of artefacts. Large, polished crystalline stone axes (the so-called *Schuhleistenkeile*) were strong enough to work timbers even as hard as oak, while small axes and chisels would have been used for more intricate work. Apart from work in the forests and in the fields, much activity may have concerned house building and furnishings, although there is little evidence in this area. However, recent discoveries of water wells with timber box-frame construction, for example at Erkenlenz-Kückhoven in Westphalia and Eythra in Saxony (Weiner 1997; Farruggia 2002), demonstrate highly skilled carpentry. Such polished stone implements were important work tools and, when necessary, they would also have made powerful weapons. They also appear to have symbolised power and prestige within the Danubian social sphere, as they were frequently placed with the dead.

While tools for heavy work tended to be made from hard rocks, smaller tools were made from various siliceous materials. Again there is variation between regions but there were clearly some common tasks which required specific tools. With the exception of arrowheads, whose use was closely associated with meat processing, and end scrapers, which seem to have been used primarily for working hide, other tool categories appear to have been put to a great variety of uses. Side scrapers were used to work hide, wood, reeds, plants, bone and antler. The so-called sickle blades, while indeed regularly employed in working plant materials and not necessarily cereals, were also used to work dry hide. Other tools, however – borers, truncated pieces and other forms – show traces of plant processing as well. Borers appear to have been the most versatile of tools, being used on wood, reeds, hide, plants, red ochre and hard gritty substances. Some analysed tools show traces of use, then of re-sharpening of the edges and subsequent reuse, not necessarily working the same materials; unworked flakes and blades also served as tools on occasion (Kuper *et al.* 1977).

The Danubians exploited a wide range of sources for the manufacture of quotidian tools. Raw materials in the area of central Europe were plentiful but not evenly distributed. Thus, some communities were able to take advantage of the proximity of raw materials to develop skills in the mining of flint and the extraction of hard rocks, and to specialise in the production of tools not only for their own needs but also for the needs of others. Today it is well established that there existed among the early farmers a vast and complex network of circulation of the various siliceous rocks and that this was based on the mining of flint and the large-scale production of semi- and finished products. Researches on the Aldenhovener Platte and in the entire Lower Rhine/Meuse area demonstrate that long distances were quite the norm; while the most commonly used raw material at the Langweiler sites was Rijckholt flint, whose

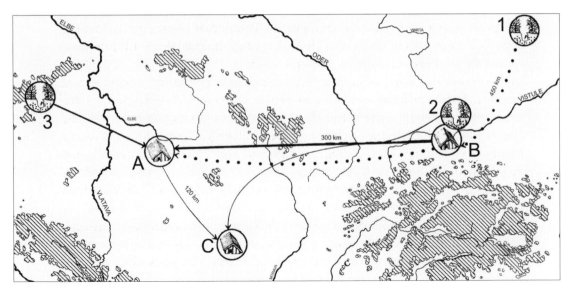

5 Exchange networks supplying raw materials to Bylany: A) Bylany; B) Olszanica; C) Vedrovice;
1) chocolate flint from Tomaszów mine; 2) Jurassic flint from Sąspów mine; 3) quartzites from
Tušimice. *Lech 1987*

sources are about 40km distant, very fine blades made of the so-called Belgian
grey flint came from as far as 170km away (Kuper *et al.* 1977; de Grooth 1991).

In the upper Rhine area the Vosges mountains offered good sources: the
nodular quartz from the vicinity of Saint Amarin was used for axe manufacture
by the *Rubané* from the end of the sixth millennium BC, while the subsequent
Rössen communities extracted pélite-quartzite in the vicinity of Plancher-les-
Mines. Numerous production villages within a radius of 10-15km from the
sources demonstrate the manufacturing process, and tools have been found up
to 150km away (the book to read and enjoy is Petrequin and Jeunesse 1995).
In the east, materials from central Polish sources, the chocolate flint from the
Holy Cross Mountains and the Jurassic-Cracow variety, were distributed over
300km or more.

Those settled far from the sources had to be enterprising in other ways:
developing and maintaining long-distance contacts that demanded time, social
effort and reciprocity. Bylany offers an excellent example of such an enterprising community: there are no known flint sources anywhere in the vicinity
and all raw material had to be obtained from a considerable distance (*5*).
Analyses from this site have identified 15 different raw materials including
Bavarian *plattensilex*, Moravský Krumlov hornstone, Tušimice quartzite (all
sources well in excess of 100km from Bylany) and, as a blade of chocolate flint
from the Holy Cross Mountains indicates, exotic items could come from much
further afield (Lech 1987).

While Danubian settlements were undoubtedly devoted primarily to a range
of domestic tasks, there is evidence of other, by no means everyday activities.

For example, areas set aside for communal feasting have been suggested for the early Danubian sites in Kujavia, with cattle and possibly wild animals providing special food for the ceremonies (Marciniak 2003). Towards the end of the LBK large earthworks make an appearance: enclosures, consisting of ditches and fences, found in association with multi-phased settlements. Sometimes, as is the case with the three Langweiler enclosures, they postdate the settlement, while elsewhere the chronological relations are uncertain (for example at Darion or Menneville). While some scholars emphasise the defensive aspect of such arrangements, the ditches often contain evidence of burials and very little of what could be classed as ordinary domestic rubbish; ritual functions, therefore, should not be overlooked.

Within the later Danubian context earthworks do not generally display such an intimate association with contemporary settlements. They also become much more formal, consisting of concentric arrangements of banks, ditches, palisades and entrances, and have a limited distribution within the heart of central Europe. The very short duration of this phenomenon – currently assessed at a century-and-a-half at the most – suggests that their creation was in response to very specific communal needs experienced by the later Danubian communities.

RELATIONS BETWEEN THE HUNTER–GATHERERS AND EARLY FARMERS

Very significantly, the late north-west European hunter-gatherers and the Danubian farmers did not live in isolation. Discoveries of items of an exotic as well as a quotidian nature originating from both contexts speak vividly for contacts, trading links and exchanges between them.

First of all, there can be little doubt that ceramic technology, so enthusias-tically adopted by some hunter-gatherer groups, was inspired by and learned through contacts with farmers. The chronologies do not support an indepen-dent origin and the use of pottery among hunter-gatherers, particularly when a degree of sedentism is involved, need not be surprising. Pottery would have fulfilled a wide range of practical functions: provision of watertight containers, improved means of cooking (especially of plant foods), safe and pest-free storage, transport of goods, relative durability and low cost are just some of the practical benefits of the use of ceramic pots, although we should not assume that organic containers were discarded. Indeed, wooden containers survive well in Denmark and the shapes and decorative patterns of some hunter-gatherer ceramics suggest the close imitation of various organic prototypes.

The social prestige of early ceramics has been discussed in archaeological literature many times and need not be repeated here, save to emphasise that the newly acquired technology as well as the possible content of the vessels (cereals and other exotic foods) would have been as important in the adoption of pottery outwith the immediate farming sphere as were the practical benefits.

Thus, from southern Scandinavia in the north to the Paris Basin in the west, several distinct ceramic traditions – the Ertebølle, Swifterbant, La Hoguette and Limbourg – have been identified with the late hunter-gatherers.

The presence of vessels with pointed bases and flat oval dishes within the Ertebølle shell-middens in Denmark has been known since the nineteenth century. Here and in Schleswig-Holstein the pottery comes from secure contexts, and there is no doubt about it being an important element of the late Mesolithic material culture. Similar ceramics are known from Dąbki on the southern Baltic coast in Poland (Ilkiewicz 1989) and from the area around the estuary of the Elbe (Schindler 1953). Recent dating of food remains from Ertebølle vessels in East Holstein indicates that pottery production began here at about 5100 BC (Hartz 1998), although it took until 4700 BC for ceramics to be made in Denmark. Between the lower Elbe and the Scheldt rivers – on the sands and in the wetlands of the Netherlands and Lower Saxony – the so-called Swifterbant pottery is present from about 4900 BC, but here the hunter-gatherers appear to have been more receptive to the novel resources, incorporating cereal growing and animal husbandry into their economy long before their Scandinavian counterparts (Raemaekers 1999).

The presence of non-Danubian ceramics on the western LBK settlements has also been known for a long time (excavations at Köln-Lindenthal). Since then, the corpus of these curious, shell- and bone-tempered vessels – with pointed bases, ovoid shapes and, often, comb-impressed decorative patterns reminiscent of basketry designs – has increased enormously and these ceramics have now been classified into two styles: the La Hoguette and the Limbourg potteries (6).

La Hoguette pottery – named after the La Hoguette cairn at Fontenay-le-Marmion, Calvados, beneath which sherds of this type were discovered – is found in the areas of the earliest Danubian presence in the west, in south-west Germany, in Alsace and in the Neckar basin, with only a sporadic presence elsewhere. The Limbourg pottery's distribution is more to the north and west, scarcely overlapping with La Hoguette: it is found on LBK sites (although not with the earliest materials) along the Meuse (Hainaut, Hesbaye, Limburg), along the lower Rhine, Rhine-Palatinate, in the Paris Basin and as far south as northern Burgundy (Constantin 1985; Jeunesse 1987, 2000; Jeunesse *et al.* 1991; Lüning *et al.* 1989; Modderman 1981; van Berg 1990).

The technology, forms and, above all, striking decoration of these ceramics make it unlikely that they should have been manufactured by the Danubian farmers who, as we have already seen, had their own assortment of vessels. Scholars generally interpret them as intrusive hunter-gatherer wares, initially inspired by contacts with the Mediterranean world of the Cardial traditions. However, while these ceramics are found in the area that is defined by the late Mesolithic industries, especially the evolved arrowheads, the unambiguous hunter-gatherer contexts are few and far between.

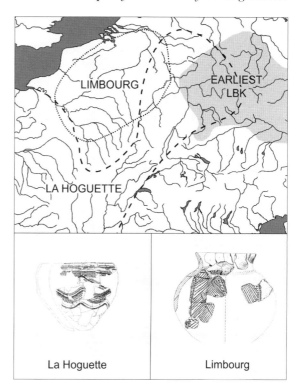

6 Distribution of La Hoguette (a) and Limbourg (b) pottery. *van Berg 1990, Lüning et al. 1998; Mazurié de Keroualin 2003*

La Hoguette pottery – which by virtue of its LBK associations should be dated from about 5500 BC – is found with late Mesolithic flint industries on a few sites, most notably at Bavans and Stuttgart-Bad Cannstatt; the latter, which is dated to 5200 BC, also contained bones of deer and ovicaprids and was apparently inhabited exclusively by the makers of La Hoguette pottery (Schütz *et al*. 1992). The Limbourg pottery, also based on associations, should not be dated to before 5300 BC, but there are no secure and unequivocal hunter-gatherer contexts for it (Mazurié de Keroualin 2003).The distribution and the sequential appearance of these two ceramic styles seem to be following the respective boundaries within the westward expansion of the LBK; it also corresponds to the left/right laterisation of the late hunter-gatherer projectiles noted earlier and may be indicative of specific population movements.

The distribution of La Hoguette also appears to be providing a possible early link between the Rhine basin and the Rhône corridor leading to the Mediterranean; in this context it is important to note the presence within the western LBK of Mediterranean plant species, namely poppy (*Papaver somniferum*) as well as flax (*Linum usitatissimum*). Thus the presence of what many consider to be hunter-gatherer ceramics on LBK settlements need not be surprising – it may not have been their pottery that the Danubian farmers were after but rather the goods inside it.

A further indication of contacts between hunter-gatherers and farmers is demonstrated within the sphere of stone and flint tools, and it is clear that influences operated in both directions, even if they continue to be geographically disparate. Perforated Danubian axes (*Schuhleistenkeile*), made of crystalline rocks, have been mapped all the way across the vast zone of the North European Plain, and deep into southern Scandinavia. Discoveries of such tools can be interpreted in a variety of ways: as strays in close proximity to the zones devoid of Danubian settlement, the adzes may indicate intermittent forays by the farmers into different landscapes, related to expeditions in search of raw materials – for example the Meuse valley sites up to 20km from the loess boundary (Louwe Kooijmans 1998), or the remarkable concentration north of the Uckermark area in Mecklenburg (Klassen 2002) – or, more realistically if found further afield, they reflect trading links and exchanges between the hunter-gatherers and the farmers.

Such axes seem to have been acquired abundantly in the western Baltic by the Ertebølle communities. While the majority are stray finds, there are sufficient numbers recovered from the Ertebølle graves and votive deposits to suggest that possession of such exotic tools was prestigious and enhanced the status of those who could procure them (Fischer 1982). Greenstone axes of central European origin are also known, albeit in smaller numbers – an interesting example of an early exotic hoard is known from Udstolpe on Lolland, where two shoe-last celts and an unperforated axe were deposited together (Lomborg 1962; Klassen 2002). Alpine jadeite and eclogite axes may have been gifts reaching Denmark sometime during the second half of the fifth millennium BC: three, unfortunately uncontexted, examples have been found on the island of Zealand (Klassen 1999, 2002).

With reference to the distribution of *Schuhleistenkeile,* it should be noted that the crossing of the Elbe in the area of modern Hamburg – identified by Bakker (1976) as one of the most important routes for the dissemination of Nordic TRB flint axes to the substantial area of the North European Plain – seems also to have served for the northward transportation of the *Schuhleistenkeile* across the Elbe, for further distribution to Holstein and the Danish islands (Klassen 2002, Fig. 20.1). One may therefore legitimately ask whether some of the so-called barrow roads across the North European Plain and in Scandinavia, with megaliths apparently their oldest markers, may not have been forged even earlier, with hunter-gatherers the first to identify easy and safe routes for transport and communication.

That tools and technologies did not move exclusively from farmers to hunter-gatherers is, however, demonstrated on the western periphery of the LBK. Here there is little evidence that the autochthonous communities were interested in the Danubian stone tools; on the contrary, it seems that it was the Mesolithic tools and technologies which were of interest to the farmers. Several studies have drawn attention to the fact that not only are the late Mesolithic arrowheads found on the earliest western LBK settlements but that, in the whole area west of the Rhine, that is in the Paris Basin and in Belgium, the

LBK communities adopt both the late Mesolithic form and the technology in the production of their armatures (Marchand 1999, 2000; Jeunesse 2000; Thévenin 1999). The adoption of indigenous forms of arrowhead was not merely a matter of technological and economic contingency but it carried with it strong social implications; indeed, as will be demonstrated later, the symbolic value of hunting in this region did not become diminished as a result of the introduction of farming.

We may point to another field of influences, undoubtedly also charged with symbolism, this time involving items of jewellery. The predilection of hunter-gatherers for personal adornment is well documented from burials (chapter 3), although such contexts may only reflect a small selection of decorative items, not preserving bodily paint, tattoos or soft-cloth fabrics. Jeunesse (2002) has convincingly argued that the predilection of certain western Danubian groups for jewellery of small marine gastropods reflects the imitation of indigenous customs, as adornment with marine shell beads was well established in the western Mesolithic.

Discoveries of amber objects in Danubian contexts on the southern fringes of the North European Plain – such as an amber zoomorphic figurine and a clay fish representation from the Lengyel site at Brześć Kujawski (7) – are considered by Polish scholars as items arriving directly from the hunter-gatherer communities of the Plain. We may also mention here the triangular decorated bone plate from Ralswiek-Augustenhof on Rügen (7). This is generally interpreted as an import from the area of Kujavia (Glob 1939; Klassen 2002); however, it could also be interpreted as a rare example of a double influence. It could well have been made in Kujavia but decorated with patterns inspired by the hunter-gatherers. While bracelets of different types (marble, schist, shell or bone) were worn by the Danubians everywhere, the decoration of the Lengyel bone bracelets from Kujavia is particularly evocative of Mesolithic designs as, indeed, are the necklaces of wild animal teeth frequently worn by the Kujavian dead (7; Czerniak 1994 and further literature quoted therein).

Perishable commodities such as plants, protein, honey and salt, skins, furs, as well as labourers and marriage partners must have crossed cultural boundaries in considerable numbers. Domesticated animals and caches of cereal undoubtedly featured in these transactions, and there is little doubt that the Breton and south Scandinavian hunter-gatherers were familiar with agricultural foodstuffs and practices. Jennbert (1984, 1998) has made a strong case for a gradual arrival of gifts of cereals within the Ertebølle contexts; the presence of *cerealia*, bracken and other light-loving species in pollen profiles along the East Holstein coasts (although not inland), dated to around the middle of the fifth millennium BC, suggests incipient forest pastures (Kalis and Meurers-Balke 1998; Hartz *et al.* 2002). Bones of domesticated animals, while not numerous, are known from this area as well.

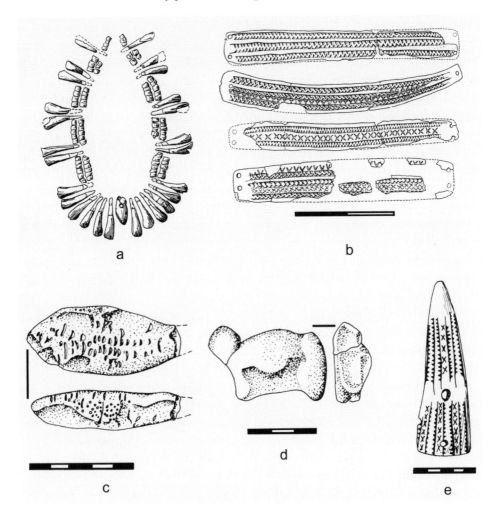

7 Decorative items from the Brześć Kujawski Lengyel group in Kujavia: a) necklace of animal teeth from a female grave at Racot; b) engraved armbands from graves at Krusza Zamkowa; c) clay fish and amber figurine from Brześć Kujawski; d) engraved bone plate from Augustenhof, Rügen. *Czerniak 1994 & 2002*

Indeed, similar scenarios have been suggested following the interpretation of pollen spectra across the north Polish lowlands (Nowak 2001). Even more dramatically, recent interpretation of the Swifterbant culture implies that communities in the area of Lower Saxony and parts of the Netherlands were very receptive and took up the challenge of agro-pastoral activities from about 4900 BC onwards (Raemaekers 1999), and Jeunesse has pointed to the precocious agricultural activities in the French Jura and on the Swiss Plateau (Jeunesse 1998). It may be equally of interest to note that micro-wear analysis on a flint blade from the late Mesolithic burial (?) pit no. 1, accompanied by a classic arrowhead of the Sonchamp type, beneath the long mound at Erdeven (Cassen *et al.* 2000, 104-5), has suggested that it was used for cutting cereals.

This discussion of contacts between the late hunter-gatherers and early farmers, while limited to selected examples, reveals that hunter-gatherers and farmers in all areas of north-western Europe were interested – in their own way and in their own time – in what their neighbours were doing. Some goods and ideas moved over long distances, perhaps rarely involving direct contact between the producers and the recipients; thus it is not certain whether many of the southern Scandinavian Ertebølle folk met face to face with Danubian farmers. In areas of closer physical proximity such contacts must have been frequent. Not all of them need have been reciprocal or friendly. Strayed Danubian cattle – as undoubtedly there would have been some – may easily have been appropriated for a Mesolithic meal (a feast?) and Keeley and Cahen (1989) have argued emphatically for a hostile rather than peaceful coexistence between hunter-gatherers and farmers in the north-west corner of the North European Plain.

CONCLUSION

We have considered a complex scenario in which groups of different cultural signatures knew one another for, in some regions, at least a millennium. A consequence of this long period of contacts and mutual influences between communities with contrasting lifestyles was the extension of the Neolithic way of life into the whole of north-west Europe. This process was neither synchronous nor uniform but it interlocked the existing cultural, economic and social phenomena into a web of dynamic relationships which led to the emergence of new cultural formations: those of the *Trichterbecherkultur* and the Cerny culture in areas which, previously, were largely the domain of hunter-gatherers.

CHAPTER TWO

EUROPE AT THE TIME OF THE LONG BARROWS – THE TRB AND CERNY CULTURES

The previous chapter outlined the cultural scene across the north-west European lowland during the sixth and earlier fifth millennia BC. It may be summarised thus: small groups of Danubian farmers residing in clearly defined ecological niches, with the remaining landscape supporting a veritable mosaic of hunting and gathering groups. Polish scholar M. Nowak has coined a very apt metaphor for such a scenario: 'small islands of farmers in the immense sea of foragers' (Nowak 2001, 590). These communities we have already seen interacting with one another across not just one but many cultural frontiers.

Against this background the appearance, outwith the Danubian sphere, of new farming communities – the TRB culture (*Trichterbecherkultur*) in the north and the Cerny culture in the west – is seen as the result of a long process of fusion of two different lifestyles. It is now appropriate to consider these new cultures themselves.

Research into the TRB culture is deeply rooted in nineteenth-century antiquarian pursuits, and the first major analysis, together with distribution maps, was published by Gustaf Kossinna at the beginning of the twentieth century. Such a long period of investigation (see Midgley 1992 for the history of TRB research) has resulted in a bewildering amount of archaeological materials and numerous scholarly treatises. The TRB thus ranks among some of the best-known and studied Neolithic cultures, even if scholarly opinion remains divided on the interpretation of this vast complex. In contrast, the Cerny culture, being a relative newcomer on the archaeological scene, cannot claim a long ancestry of research, although the speed with which new materials have come to light is quite staggering. First 'signposted' by Gerard Bailloud at the 1961 Atlantic Colloquium in Brest, Cerny was defined by him three years later, principally on the basis of material from less than a dozen sites (Bailloud

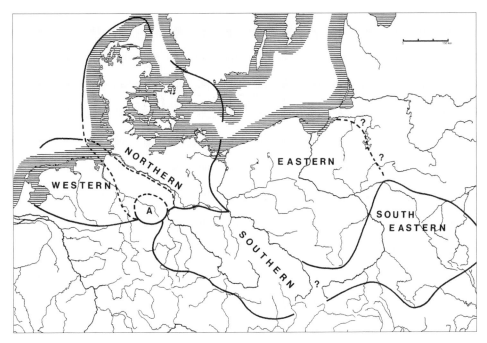

8 Distribution of the TRB culture. *Midgley 1992*

1964, 61-73). Thirty years later, the site catalogue accompanying the proceedings of the 1994 Colloquium at Nemours listed 235 definite sites belonging to
the Cerny culture. If, in addition, one considers the whole range of central and
western Cerny-related ceramic styles, this cultural complex is today quite
substantial (Constantin *et al.* 1997).

The TRB culture, in its ultimate extent, covered most of the area from the
present-day Netherlands in the west to central and eastern Poland in the east,
and from southern Scandinavia in the north to Bohemia and Moravia in the
south. Because of this geographical vastness, as well as varied scholarly attitudes,
regional studies have always been the hallmark of research, and several geographically discrete groups have been distinguished (*8*). In contrast, the Cerny culture
covers a much smaller area, principally that of northern France. Its heart lies in
the south Paris Basin, especially in the Seine and Yonne river valleys, and it is
found from Normandy and the Channel Islands in the north to Charente in
the south and, more sparsely, in Picardy and Champagne to the east (*9*). While
less clear, the relationship with the Breton materials – especially the so-called
Castellic tradition – suggests at least a considerable influence of the Cerny
tradition upon the west. French scholars also distinguish several regional groups:
for example Cerny *éponyme*, Cerny-Barbuise, Chambon etc. (Constantin *et al.*
1997), but these could be considered as much in terms of different ceramic
styles as regional groups characteristic of the TRB culture.

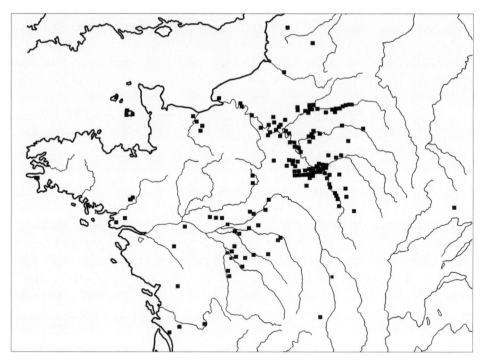

9 Distribution of the Cerny culture. *Constantin* et al. *1997*

THE CHRONOLOGY OF THE TRB AND THE CERNY CULTURES

The relative chronologies of the TRB and the Cerny cultures are based primarily upon the analysis of ceramic styles. These are well established in all the regions of the TRB culture (Midgley 1992, chapter 4), but less so in the Cerny where, as noted above, the different ceramic styles may represent regional *facies* as much as chronological sequences. The principal difficulties in establishing absolute chronologies are related to the small number of radio-carbon dates, especially from the transitional and early periods, as well as to the ambiguities of calibration.

On present evidence the chronology of the TRB culture is complex. In its cradle, that is in the area from Kujavia in the east to Lower Saxony in the west, the crystallisation of the TRB culture should be dated to 4500/4400 BC, and it clearly took several centuries before it manifested itself further north. Dates from Schleswig-Holstein suggest the presence of the TRB from about 4200 BC, and in Denmark perhaps a little later, 4000–3900 BC.

While in typo-chronological terms the Cerny culture follows on from the Villeneuve-Saint-Germain late Danubian group, there is a lack of radiocarbon dates for the early phase. The most recent reassessment of C-14 dates from the Paris Basin (Dubouloz 2003) suggests that the majority of the Cerny dates centre around 4550-4500/4350-4300 BC; for the time being it is not unreasonable to suggest the emergence of the Cerny culture some time prior to 4500 BC. Indeed, barring differences in the intricacies of regional development, the general synchronicity of the Cerny and the TRB cultures is in keeping with the process of transition from the late Danubian to the subsequent Neolithic cultures.

The demise of the TRB culture sometime between 2900 and 2700 BC was, like its origins, a complex process; it is poorly documented in the archaeological record and its interpretation remains largely intuitive. In global terms the TRB culture was followed by another massive, pan-European phenomenon, that of the largely pastoral Corded Ware culture, although the situation is complicated by the presence of small regional complexes, such as the Globular Amphora culture on the North European Plain or the Pitted Ware culture in southern Scandinavia. The end of the Cerny culture is similarly ambivalent, although it was of much shorter duration. On present evidence it seems to have been followed, within five to six centuries, by a whole range of small regional groupings such as Noyen and Balloy and, within a broader regional context, by the Chasséen culture sometime after the transition from the fifth and fourth millennia BC.

There is no suggestion here that the TRB and the Cerny cultures are closely connected or that one had any considerable influence upon the other, although extraordinary similarities in some items from both cultures inspire tantalising thoughts on direct, if sporadic, contacts. Rather, the two cultures display a number of characteristics which imply that the process of their emergence – largely outwith the area of the earlier Danubian tradition – and the trajectories of their social, economic and technological development followed a similar course. By way of illustrating some of these phenomena we may consider aspects of settlement and industrial development. The ceremonial landscape, which provided a permanent and dramatic setting for social interaction and expression of ritual beliefs, will be discussed later.

THE TRB CULTURE

Land use and settlement

In contrast to the Danubians, the TRB farmers had a strong preference for lighter soils, locating their settlements in hilly landscapes interspersed with bogs, marshes and stretches of open water. Such topography emphasised the importance of both the dry, higher ground and the low-lying, wetter landscape; it also ensured ecological diversity with a combination of forest, meadow and arable land offering ideal conditions for early agriculture. The only reliable evidence of agricultural activities comes from the presence of cereal crops and bones of domesticated animals on settlement sites. However, it was the Danish palaeobotanist J. Iversen who, in the 1940s, first recognised the possibility of interpreting man's influence on the natural environment through the study of pollen records. Subsequent research in this field, using pollen spectra from bog deposits and from old land surfaces preserved beneath the burial mounds, has led to an understanding of the type and extent of anthropogenic activities of the early farmers settled on the North European Plain and in southern Scandinavia. (Midgley 1992, chapter 8, offers a general discussion of environmental aspects in northern Europe.)

Recent analyses of pollen profiles from northern and central Poland – from areas outwith the Danubian enclaves, and dating to before the middle of the fifth millennium BC – show considerable management of natural environments by human agencies. The combination of traces of charcoal, charred vegetation and the presence of light-loving species indicate sophisticated management of deciduous woodland, based on a combination of fire and coppicing, and points to the deliberate maintenance of a more open environment. Pollen diagrams from the subsequent period, after 4500 BC, show that this forest management activity intensifies: apart from the continued presence of light-loving species, *Cerealia, Hordeum t.* and *Plantago lanceolata* make an appearance, and a similar situation is witnessed on a number of sites further inland in northern and central Poland (Nowak 1999, 53–56).

Similarly, pollen diagrams from the coastal regions in East Holstein reveal, prior to the mid-fifth millennium BC, deliberate and increasing forest utilisation (Kalis and Meurers-Balke 1998; Hartz *et al.* 2000). Light-loving species and, in particular, the persistent presence of *Pteridium* are taken as an indication of deliberate forest burning and coppicing in order to maintain light conditions. From 4200 BC cereals appear in a number of Holstein diagrams on the coast as well as inland; this evidence is given further gravitas by the identification of charred emmer grains from a sherd at Wangels, accompanied at this site by cereal processing implements in the form of grinding stones (Hartz *et al.* 2000, 137). Further north, pollen data from various localities in Scania, eastern Denmark and north Jutland show that in the early TRB period (EN in the Scandinavian nomenclature) open lime or birch forests were maintained for small-scale cultivation and intensive grazing of cattle and pig; in the later TRB (MN period) coppiced hazel woodlands were used for permanent cereal growing, with repeated burnings for the improvement of grazing (Andersen S.Th. 1988, 1990, 1995).

Such activities, apparent in the pollen record from at least 4700 BC, must have been initiated by the late Mesolithic communities. They demonstrate a very intimate relationship with the various natural environments, based on understanding of the complexity of nature. Maintaining an open forest environment attractive to game plays an important role in successful hunting, and may subsequently have been conducive to forest grazing of domesticated animals and to garden-like cereal cultivation. Against this background the incorporation of cereals and domesticated animals into the traditional economy

– whether they were acquired as gifts or resulted from exchanges with the Danubian farmers – was simply an additional dimension within the already diverse economy.

The actual economic data from the transition period are still inadequate; nevertheless there is some support for the picture offered by the environmental sources. The late Mesolithic site at Dudka, north-eastern Poland, was located in a landscape described by the excavators as a paradise for hunting and fishing but, towards the end of the occupation, the domesticated pig makes an appearance (Gumiński 1998; Gumiński and Fiedorczuk 1990). The Ertebølle site at Dąbki, on the Polish Baltic coast, sees an increase in cattle consumption, from 6 per cent to 23 per cent of animal bones towards the end of the settlement period (Ilkiewicz 1989). New research from Holstein confirms the early dating of the domesticated cattle bones from the Ertebølle layers at Rosenhof (between 4900 and 4500 BC; Hartz *et al.* 2000, 136), although it is still difficult to connect this evidence with subsequent developments and we need to await the final analyses of materials from this site. The coastal site of Wangels is dated to the period from 4300 to 3900 BC. Here, in addition to the above-mentioned evidence for the use of cereals, domesticated animals (cattle, sheep/goat and a very small amount of pig) were also present, accounting for 63 per cent of the analysed bones, but hunting of wild species and fishing of marine as well as freshwater fish continued (Heinrich 1998).

Even in Denmark, where the transition from the Mesolithic to the Neolithic way of life has generally been argued to be fairly swift, new evidence suggests that the process may have been more gradual. Excavations at Visborg, on the north shore of the Mariager Fjord in Jutland, have brought to light a coastal kitchen midden site which dates to the final Ertebølle and the earliest TRB. While only brief preliminary reports are available at the moment (Andersen S.H. 1998; 2000a) they show that during the early TRB period hunting, fishing, sealing and fowling continued but that, alongside these traditional pursuits, a few domesticates - cattle and pigs - were kept; small quantities of cereal pollen suggest some crop-growing as well. A similar slow process of transition has been observed in Store Åmose (Fischer 1985, Stafford 1999) and a number of scholars have argued for quite some time for a more gradual process of incorporation of domesticates into the traditional economy (Jennbert 1984, 1998; Andersen S.H. 2000a).

Once fully established, the TRB culture economy was based on mixed farming, that is, cereal growing and animal husbandry, supplemented by hunting and gathering. All the basic cereals appear to have been cultivated: among the wheats emmer (*Triticum dicoccum*) and einkorn (*Triticum monococcum*) represent the main varieties and are found throughout the whole area of the TRB; barley was present in two varieties, six-row barley (*Hordeum vulgare*) and two-row naked barley (*Hordeum distichum*) and, being more resistant to cold and suited to cultivation on mixed lowland soils, it increased in importance towards the end of the TRB. Leguminous plants, such as peas (*Pisum sativum*), lentils (*Lens culinaris*) and beans (*Vicia faba*) appear regularly, albeit not in large quantities, and flax (*Linum usitatissimum*) may have been grown not only for the oil in the seeds but also for its fibre (Midgley 1992, chapter 8).

Although they rarely survive in the archaeological record, a great variety of wild plants would have been gathered throughout the seasons to provide nourishment and medicines and to add variety to the diet. Edible forest fungi were undoubtedly gathered – as they are to this day – in the forests across the North European Plain. Apples, raspberries, cherries, plums and elderberries have been found on some sites, and plants such as sorrel (*Rumex*) and wild garlic (*Allium ursinum*) may have been grown as vegetables (Kruk 1980, List I and II).

Among the domesticated animals, cattle were by far the most important everywhere, followed by pig, with sheep and goat generally appearing in the animal bone assemblages in much smaller quantities. Cattle predominate on settlement sites but, interestingly, pigs may have been important in communal feasting since their bones are found in larger numbers within ditches of ceremonial enclosures in southern Scandinavia, for example at Toftum and Troldebjerg. In this context the site of Sarup on Fyn provides an interesting example, in spite of relatively small overall bone assemblages: pig was consumed more while the site functioned as a ceremonial enclosure (33 per cent in phase I and 66 per cent in phase II) than when it became a settlement (23 per cent in phase III; Andersen N.H. 1997, 112).

Apart from providing meat, domesticated animals were, of course, a source of other materials: skins for clothing, wool for garments, milk for dairy products and bone for tools. Cattle, significantly, could be used to provide pulling power. While archaeo-zoological evidence for this activity is rather sparse within the TRB, vessel iconography (for example, the celebrated pot from Bronocice with images of a wheeled vehicle), the wheel tracks from under a barrow at Flintbek near Kiel, and the numerous plough-marks preserved under the north European barrows suggest that cattle were used as draught animals (Midgley 1992, 378; Bakker *et al.* 1999). Indeed, over ten years ago, Bogucki (1993, 501) urged archaeologists not to overlook the lowly oxen when interpreting strategies for the acquisition of wealth, power and prestige practised by the Neolithic communities.

Cereals and domesticated animals were the mainstay of the TRB economy, but hunting and gathering, while its role should not be exaggerated, continued. Indeed, many hunting and fishing stations established during the late Mesolithic remained in use throughout most of the TRB. The lake belt of the north European lowland offered favourable conditions for such activities: fish remains are well represented at Hüde on the Dümmer lake in Lower Saxony, and at Bistoft near Flensburg in Schleswig-Holstein; at Ustowo, a late TRB site in Poland, nearly 40 per cent of animal bones belong to wild species, with deer, bison and wild boar being most common. Further north, in Store

Åmose, Zealand, farmers continued to use the previous hunting and fishing locations. The small island of Hesselø, north of Zealand, was popular during the winter months with seal hunters and Sølager, by the Roskilde Fjord, may have been a fishing outpost for those living at Havnelev, 3km further inland; it was also used to catch winter migrating birds. The old shell-middens continued to be occupied; at Norsminde, Bjørnsholm and Visborg there is evidence of farming settlement just outside the main midden zone, suggesting that permanent occupation was possible along the coast.

The constant, if variable, presence of wild animals within the TRB suggests that, as during the late Mesolithic, hunting also fulfilled an important social role. Indeed, teeth of wild animals, boars' tusks and fish vertebrae continued to inspire craftsmen in the manufacture of personal jewellery. The ornaments placed in the graves at the Mecklenburg cemetery at Ostorf are an eloquent testimony to the importance of hunting trophies as expressions of a world view in which the wild played an important role (chapter 6).

Initially, the TRB settlements appear to have been small and of a fleeting nature, although this may reflect the preservation conditions since many early sites are found preserved under earthen long barrows. A number of Scandinavian sites, including the famous Barkær site on the Djursland peninsula once thought to be classic Danubian-style long houses, have now been convincingly reinterpreted as long barrows placed upon early TRB settlements. The actual settlement structures are, however, difficult to interpret. The Sarnowo cemetery (chapter 4) was most probably founded when the inhabitants chose to move onto the slightly higher and drier land directly to the north of the original location. Foundations of small rectangular houses, together with traces of an ancient ploughed field, have been found underneath the earthen mounds; similar houses were subsequently built further up the slope. While scholarly opinion with respect to the ploughed field at this site is strongly divided, some of the later Danish mounds were unarguably placed upon previously cultivated fields, with plough-marks surviving under the protection of the mounds. Light buildings of uncertain construction have been noted at Łącko in Kujavia, Mosegården in Jutland and Lindebjerg on Zealand, and D-shaped houses postulated at Hanstedgård in Jutland and possibly at Troldebjerg on Langeland (Midgley 1992, chapter 7).

Only when the TRB culture became fully established do we witness the presence of larger sites. The late TRB settlement at Spodsbjerg on Langeland apparently extended over 300,000 square metres, while that at Bronocice, southeast Poland, is estimated to have covered about 500,000 square metres, even if traces of the actual houses continue to be elusive. Other large sites include the upland settlements in central Germany, such as Wallendorf and the ditched and palisaded site at Dölauer Heide (Midgley 1992, 320). House structures really only become clear towards the end of the TRB, for example the rectangular houses at Flögeln, near Cuxhaven, and at Wittenwater, near Uelzen.

Occasionally the locations seem to have been quite challenging. The late TRB sites on the island of Bornholm are a remarkable testimony to the navigational skills of the Neolithic farmers. The 37km-wide strait separating this island from the Swedish mainland is known for its very strong currents and changing winds, and the crossing must have been one of the most hazardous enterprises of that time. Excavations on the southern part of the island, at Limensgård and Grødbygård, have brought to light remarkable remains of several long, rectangular TRB houses, up to 22m in length, revealing sophisticated architecture based on complex arrangements of central and side posts supporting the roofs of the structures (Nielsen and Nielsen 1985).

The TRB pottery

The TRB pottery is one of the commonest and most frequently encountered elements of the material culture (*colour plate 4*). Its strongly decorative character has, from the very beginning, lent itself to typo-chronological analyses which led to the definition of numerous regional groupings (Midgley 1992, chapter 4). While such studies have helped towards the understanding of the developmental sequence of ceramic style and the relative chronology of the TRB culture in different regions, they tended to obscure the fact that pottery became an important symbolic resource employed in numerous areas of social life. While the Danubian ceramics appear to have belonged by and large to the domestic scene, the TRB pottery, from the very beginning, was used in a wide range of contexts, extending well beyond the domestic arena. Thus, as a part of votive activities, vessels were deposited in bogs, at the edges of lakes, or in the enclosures; they also played a significant role in funerary rituals, both as grave goods and in ancestral ceremonies which involved placement of large quantities of pots either within or outside the tombs.

The bog deposits are a classic example of a ritual use of ceramics, and this tradition may have had roots in the Mesolithic beliefs associated with the symbolic significance of lakes and rivers. TRB vessels, placed in what originally were margins of lakes and other watery locations, are known across the whole of the North European Plain, although many of the finds are poorly documented. Such finds are known from Poland and Mecklenburg (a famous and initially large deposit found at Gingst, on the island of Rügen, survives only as a small collection of vessels at the Stralsund museum) but, being mostly accidental discoveries, are not very well documented. Beakers described by Schwabedissen as characteristic of his Satrup phase (Schwabedissen 1958) in reality may well be examples of such votive offerings, since many have been collected from different localities on Satrupholm Moor.

The tradition of bog pots is, however, very well documented in eastern Denmark. Records for bog pots brought to light through peat cutting go as far back as the 1870s, and there was a conscious effort on the part of archaeologists – museum curators and amateurs alike – to preserve and document as many finds as possible. An excellent recent publication of bog-pot analysis from eastern Denmark by Eva Koch (1998) records 688, vessels of which 671 can be attributed to the TRB; the famous Store Åmose area in central Zealand, where regular offerings were made throughout the TRB period near the original edge of the large lake, has yielded 297 pots and numerous other finds, as well as evidence of ritual constructions.

The tradition of votive offerings at the edges of lakes may well have begun during the late Ertebølle: axes made of flint, stone and deer antler (some decorated), amber beads and other late Mesolithic items have been found in a number of locations where, subsequently, TRB deposits had been placed. Koch's study of the Neolithic bog pots suggests that, while the votive offerings were being made throughout the entire duration of the TRB, they varied considerably: the most intensive votive deposits date to the period from 3500 to 2950 BC, and coincide with the period of other ritual activities such as the construction of megalithic tombs and the ceremonial use of the causewayed enclosures (Koch 1998, 172).

Several aspects of these lake deposits are of interest. Firstly, the vast majority of vessels (89 per cent) represent the commonest domestic category, that of the beaker. At least some were used for cooking prior to their deposition in the water: traces of fish meals have been identified on a few interiors, and staining of the exterior walls suggests foodstuffs which had boiled over (*ibid*. 151). Additionally, some pots were placed in the same locations as animal bones. Initially, wild species predominated but later domesticated animals became quite common. Quite exceptional finds include complete skeletons of domesticated cattle such as those found at Store Åmose; and at Jordløse Mose XXII two beakers of an early form were found close to a clearly arranged and stone-covered deposit of bones of six cattle together with remains of sheep, goat, red and roe deer, bird, fish and domesticated dog (*ibid*. 305-54, 363).

Another significant aspect is the spatial relationship to other types of site. Spatial analysis undertaken in some localities has long suggested that deposits of axe hoards in waterlogged environments were in close proximity to megalithic tombs (Ebbesen 1982). Koch's analysis of the bog deposits takes this relationship further: a majority of bog pots are within a radius of 1km from known settlement sites and/or from megalithic tombs (Koch 1998, 139-40, Figs. 108-11). Such a relationship between land sites and watery ritual deposits, combined with the use of quotidian materials – be they foodstuffs or daily implements such as cooking vessels – highlights the symbolic relationship between the man-made and natural landscapes.

Another area of social activity in which pottery played an important role is represented through ceremonies associated with burials, commemorations of the dead and ancestral rituals which involved the use of causewayed enclosures and burial monuments. While causewayed enclosures were associated with a wide range of rituals, only some of which related directly to burial, pottery was used and subsequently deposited here in a range of contexts: complete vessels were placed against timber fences, whole or fragmented in ditches and in the interior pits. From Sarup on the island of Fyn – the most fully published TRB causewayed enclosure to date (Andersen N.H. 1997) – we know that the most commonly used ceramic forms were beakers and the so-called Troldebjerg bowls.

While pots, together with other items such as flint axes, amber or copper beads, accompanied the dead inside the burial chambers, by far the most dramatic employment of ceramics in southern Scandinavia was their deposition and destruction in front of the tombs (Bagge and Kaelas 1950; Kjærum 1969; Skaarup 1985). This phenomenon, which began on a relatively modest scale, reached its maximum at the time of the Troldebjerg and Blandebjerg ceramic styles. In many instances the stylistic homogeneity of the ceramics suggests only one or two ceremonies conducted in front of the ancestral tomb. Vessels chosen for such offerings were richly decorated and appear to have been selected specially for this purpose, with manufacture geared to ritual rather than domestic activity. They comprise a much wider range of forms than those which made up the bog offerings; apart from beakers, bowls of different kinds, pedestalled bowls and clay spoons were also included.

While hundreds of vessels were placed and subsequently destroyed in front of the south Scandinavian tombs, in the western TRB – in Lower Saxony and the Netherlands – vast numbers of pots were placed in the interior of the chambers as part of a related ritual. Although Bakker has noted that finds of broken pots were made to the side of the entrance in a number of Dutch tombs and may well represent a tradition similar to that from Scandinavia (Bakker 1992, 58), the profusion of ceramics in the interior of some of the Western chambers is quite staggering: 649 TRB pots were deposited in the Havelte D53 tomb, while Emmeln 2 contained 1,200 vessels. Moreover, as Bakker noted, typical settlement forms such as 'baking plates and robust storage funnel beakers' were extremely rare in megalithic chambers (*ibid.* 57).

Thus, pottery in the North European Neolithic fulfilled an important social and ceremonial role, and the virtual explosion in ceramic forms and swiftly changing decorative styles has to be seen against the background of social rather than domestic needs. Indeed, evidence from southern Scandinavia suggests that, on occasion, pottery may have been produced en masse during large public gatherings and more or less immediately disposed of through communal feasting or other rituals; the making of the vessels may in itself have been an important communal act.

The flint industries

The circulation of commodities in Neolithic northern Europe initially followed the older Mesolithic routes, but soon developed into a vast communication and exchange network covering the whole of southern Scandinavia and the European lowland. While hard crystalline rocks, typical of the Danubian complexes, were used in the TRB for items of ceremonial display such as battle axes, the high level of Mesolithic expertise in the use of flint was applied to the development of a new kind of industry catering for the needs of farmers. This involved considerable investment in mining and mass production of a variety of flint tools.

Major flint extraction centres of the TRB culture developed in the vicinity of the geographically limited primary flint sources: the Holy Cross Mountains of Poland were the source of the so-called 'chocolate', Świeciechów and the banded Krzemionki flint; the northern Danish and southern Swedish sources provided the Danian and Kristianstad flint types; and the island of Rügen was exploited for its primary deposits along the Baltic sea cliffs (Midgley 1992, 132-5). Evidence from Poland – for example from the workshops discovered at the settlement sites of Ćmielów and Świeciechów – shows that individual craftsmen could work different kinds of flint with equal ease (Balcer 1975), while workshops at Kvarnby, southern Scania, demonstrate the very wide range of forms produced (Rudebeck 1987).

The polished flint axe is a *tour de force* of this industry: it is clearly of local origin, with Mesolithic flake axes providing the most convincing prototypes. North Jutland appears to have had a monopoly in the provision of axes to the western part of the European lowland, while the Polish and Rügen sources supplied the rest of the area. Not only were the axe manufacturing centres able to satisfy the seemingly continuous demand for axes as tools, but they produced a surplus which could easily be taken out of circulation. Like pottery, flint axes were an important social resource and were employed in a variety of social and ceremonial contexts.

The significance of the TRB axe hoards (*colour plate 5*), either from watery or dry-land locations, has been the subject of many analyses and their results need not be repeated here (Nielsen 1984, Rech 1979). It is nevertheless interesting to note that in northern Europe the deposition of axes – of flint, stone or antler – commences in the context of the late Mesolithic Ertebølle culture (Koch 1998, 157-158) and that the increase of this activity in the Neolithic must represent a transformation – to use Bradley's phrase (1998, xviii) – of an already existing tradition onto a new, massive scale and in altered social conditions. Just as for pottery, an essential everyday tool such as the flint axe has also become an important social resource with high symbolic prestige, employed in complex inter-communal exchanges and freely disposed of in waterlogged locations, at megalithic tombs and in causewayed enclosures.

It hardly needs emphasising that the same routes that facilitated the dissemination of axes offered opportunities for the movement of other commodities. The use of amber for personal adornment is also deeply rooted in the Mesolithic tradition – zoomorphic amber figurines were one of the earliest commodities exchanged between the hunter-gatherers and the Danubian farmers – and amber in the form of beads, discs and miniature battle axes were made and used in large quantities. The battle axe in Nordic mythology was a symbol of a deity associated with thunder, rain and water: since amber appears on the shore precisely under such conditions, this 'origin' may well have made amber a very desirable commodity.

THE CERNY CULTURE

Settlement and land use

The Cerny communities had an equally strong preference for lighter soils, locating their settlements in hilly areas, with upland locations indicating a new approach to the exploitation of landscapes. In the south Paris Basin, especially along the Seine and Yonne river valleys, the palaeochannels – reflecting the ancient river meanders – suggest that the low-lying plains were subject to seasonal flooding. As on the North European Plain, the topography of landscapes settled by the Cerny emphasises the importance of both the drier, higher ground and the low-lying, wetter landscape, ensuring ecological diversity with a combination of forest, pastoral meadow and arable land providing suitable conditions for agriculture.

Evidence for cereal cultivation is rather sparse, although a Mediterranean crop unknown to the LBK farmers, naked wheat (*Triticum aestivo-compactum*), has been identified on a number of sites. Thus in the Loire valley, at Fossé and at Contres, it has been found with hazelnuts and acorns, and at Muides with barley (*Hordeum sp.*); on the Plaine de Caen, at Ernes, it was also accompanied by hazelnuts (Hamon *et al.* 1997; Chancerel *et al.* 1992). Consideration of a curious ceramic form – flat clay discs, known in the Cerny as *plats à pain* but equally well represented in the TRB – is of interest here. Those of the Cerny culture are thought to have derived from the south, perhaps accompanying the northward spread of naked wheat. This wheat is more suitable for baking than other wheat varieties. There are no analyses of food residue from these ceramic forms, but the name *plats à pain* may well reflect their function, suggesting that the French, as well as the north European, tradition of bread baking may have a very long ancestry indeed.

On the other hand, Augereau (1993) has suggested that the relative scarcity of cereal processing tools on the Cerny sites in the south Paris Basin indicates a secondary role of crops in this area, and that the main focus of the economy was animal husbandry. Recent research on animal bone assemblages from the same area suggests that, indeed, the economy may have been geared to cattle rearing, with other species playing a less significant role. Tresset (1996) has analysed animal bone assemblages from the Cerny enclosures at Balloy, Barbuise-Courtavant and Châtenay. Cattle were by far the most important, accounting for up to 80 per cent of the domesticated species, with pig varying from between 15 and 20 per cent and with a negligible contribution from sheep and goats. She has argued for the management of livestock that was geared principally towards meat consumption, although the specific nature of the enclosed sites – with ceremonial functions that may have involved communal feasting – and the clear symbolic significance of cattle, as demonstrated through ritual deposits in the enclosure ditches, cautions against extending such a pattern to all other sites. Indeed, faunal assemblages from the Loire valley and from Normandy, while not large, offer a more eclectic image.

We have already noted the importance of hunting within the TRB culture and this activity seems to have been equally important in the Cerny, albeit with an interesting difference. Bone assemblages suggest that, at least in some regions, red deer stags and male wild boars were specifically targeted. The contribution of such selective hunting to the overall economy would have been negligible in terms of food provision but, as in northern Europe, its symbolic and social role is very dramatically documented within the funerary sphere (chapter 5).

In considering the settlement of the Cerny culture we need to bear in mind that most sites have come to light as a result of rescue projects and, often, only small areas have been excavated. An equally important factor lies in the preoccupation of French researchers with the notion of settlement defence. This may be reflected in the choice of location, for example on a promontory, or in the presence of ditch and palisade structures enclosing sites located on the valley floors. Upland sites have been excavated but only two – the eponymous Cerny '*Parc aux Bœufs*' (Essonne) with its undated stone wall, and Boulancourt '*le Châtelet*' (Seine-et-Marne) with a short stretch of palisade trench – have revealed any structures that could be regarded as defensive in nature (Mordant and Simonin 1997). Evidence from most other sites consists either of surface finds or series of pits and hearths, with domestic architecture difficult to identify; even in cases where old land surfaces have survived well under subsequent burial cairns, for example at Colombiers-sur-Seulles and Ernes in Normandy, settlement traces are ephemeral to say the least.

However, on rare occasions structures have been identified. Trapezoidal foundations – evoking the preceding Villeneuve-Saint-Germain architectural tradition – have been found on a number of sites: at Molinons in the Yonne valley, at Marolles-sur-Seine (*10*; Mordant and Mordant 1970) and at Herblay, in the Oise valley (Valais 1995); a small quadrilateral structure defined by post holes was found at Pont-Sainte-Maxence, Oise (Prodeo *et al.* 1997).

At the upland site of Herblay, in addition to the trapezoidal building, there was also a circular structure identified from a setting of 18 post holes on a 7.5m diameter. Indeed, in recent years, circular buildings have been considered as another possible type of Cerny house (*11*). Two similar structures have been found at Orval (Cher; Verjux 1999b), respectively 18m and 14m in diameter, each with one entry and the interior divided into two parts; an aerial

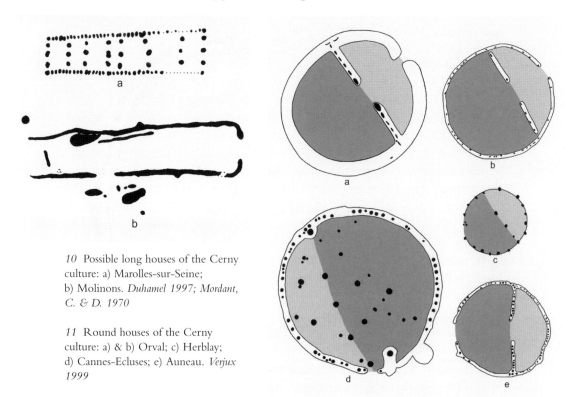

10 Possible long houses of the Cerny culture: a) Marolles-sur-Seine; b) Molinons. *Duhamel 1997; Mordant, C. & D. 1970*

11 Round houses of the Cerny culture: a) & b) Orval; c) Herblay; d) Cannes-Ecluses; e) Auneau. *Verjux 1999*

photograph of the Beaumont enclosure revealed a circular structure of about 12m in diameter, with an internal partition into two unequal parts. Recent excavations at Auneau (Eure-et-Loire; Verjux 1999b) included that of a structure defined by a roughly circular foundation trench 11.5m in diameter with a gap of 2.5m in the west wall. The distribution of finds suggested that flint was worked close to the entrance and that cooking took place further inside the building.

Association of these circular structures with the Cerny culture requires confirmation through further discoveries and clarification of chronological and contextual relations. However, if correct, it would reflect a situation similar to that on the North European Plain – a dramatic break with the Danubian long-house tradition. Mesolithic houses are yet to be discovered in northern France but they may well have contributed to the Cerny domestic architecture.

Many enclosed sites, resulting from excavations as well as from aerial reconnaissance projects, have been identified in France. As elsewhere in Europe, enclosures have been constructed over a long period of time and therefore only excavated sites can be attributed to particular cultures. Nevertheless, the identifiable Cerny enclosures are subject to very different interpretations. In the area of the Yonne and Seine river valleys several sites have been partially investigated, for example Barbuise-Courtavant, Châtenay-sur-Seine and Villeneuve-

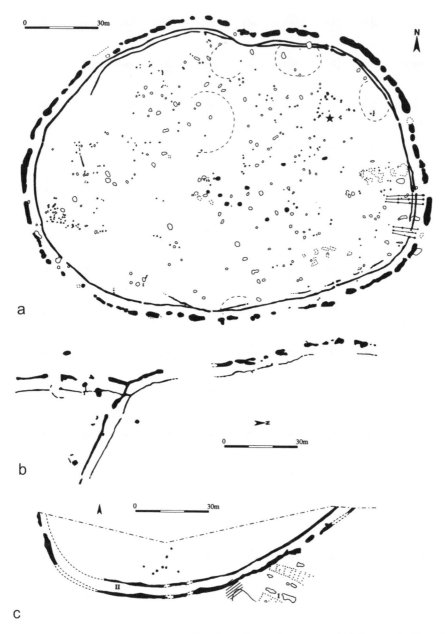

12 Enclosures of the Cerny culture: a) Balloy; b) Barbuise-Courtavant; c) Villeneuve-la-Guyard. *Mordant & Simonin 1997*

la-Guyard, but only one, at Balloy, has been excavated completely (*12*; Mordant and Simonin 1997; Augereau and Mordant 1993; Mordant 1991; Mordant 1997).

The sites display certain regularities in terms of their sub-circular or oval form, in their location along the obvious communication routes and in their physical proximity to flowing water. Some are very intimately associated with monumental cemeteries (chapters 4 and 6). The ditches, which may be continuous or segmented, are generally associated with internal palisades. At Barbuise-Courtavant alterations to the layout of the ditch and palisade suggest some remodelling, perhaps leading to an increase in the enclosed area. At Villeneuve-la-Guyard a 150m stretch of the Cerny enclosure – consisting of a continuous ditch with an elaborate entrance and a palisade – survived modern quarrying; the ditch was thought to be too small to fulfil any defensive needs (Prestreau 1992).

Only the enclosure at Balloy, totally excavated under the direction of Daniel Mordant, provides evidence lending itself to interpretation; certain aspects pertinent to the use of this site will be elaborated later. The Balloy enclosure, which partly overlay an earlier settlement of the VSG culture, is in the form of a rough oval of 167m by 123m. It consists of about 60 discontinuous segments and an inner palisade which respects the layout of the ditch segments; a second inner palisade enclosed an area reduced in size at the western part. While the interior as well as the ditch segments contained large quantities of material – pottery, flint and animal bones – there were no features that could be interpreted as houses. The only structures which could have had a domestic function were the so-called *structures de combustion* – shallow pits with traces of burning which yielded many fragments of grindstones. Among the pottery sherds 150 handles with horizontal perforations were thought to be indicative of storage vessels.

Balloy was interpreted as an example of an enclosed Cerny village, but all the activities carried out in the enclosure – and this includes the preparation and cooking of food – could equally have been conducted as part of ceremonial practices. Many of the finds from the ditches have a distinctly symbolic character – cattle jaws arranged to look like a set of horns placed on a layer of broken pottery, ox skulls, finely decorated and deliberately broken vessels. If one emphasises the intimate relationship of this enclosure with the nearby monumental cemetery, its symbolic function speaks more powerfully than the domestic function assigned by the excavator. Indeed, such an interpretation would be entirely in keeping with evidence from other contemporary European contexts.

Cerny ceramics

As elsewhere, in everyday life the Cerny pottery was used for storing, cooking and serving food. It was well made, with burnt bone as the main tempering agent evoking connection with the La Hoguette and Limbourg ceramics discussed previously (chapter 1). Decoration was carried out using pointed tools, spatulae and multiple-tooth combs and comprised a wide assortment of motifs combining vertical and horizontal designs; meanders and garlands were particularly common.

Constantin remarked that, in comparison with the Danubian vessels, the Cerny forms increased in size. Thus bowls – of which nearly 90 percent are decorated – became larger (their volume varying between 1.2 and 6.5 litres) and many seem to have been made for collective rather than just individual use. The profuse decoration and the strip handles, attached at the widest point, emphasise the presentational aspect of such vessels (Constantin 1997, 67) and their frequent discoveries in the ditches of enclosed sites suggest that they may have been used for serving food to large gatherings.

Evidence available to date makes it difficult to comment on the employment of the Cerny ceramics outwith the purely domestic sphere. It is difficult, for example, to discern the nature of pottery that has been dredged from the Seine and the Loire rivers: are these vessels washed out from the riverine settlements or should we consider them as possible examples of votive deposits, similar in nature to those known from northern Europe?

A curious and pertinent example is offered by the so-called square-mouthed (*vases à bouche carrée*) or 'deliberately deformed' ceramics, found on settlements – especially frequently within the south Cerny Chambon group of the Loire region – as well as in the Cerny graves (*13* and *colour plate 19*; chapter 5). Square-mouthed vessels are characteristic of the fifth millennium BC north Italian VBQ culture (*vasi a bocca quadrata*), although examples are found throughout most of western Europe (Bazzanella 1997). In general, the discussion of this pottery has centred on possible inter-cultural contacts, but since the

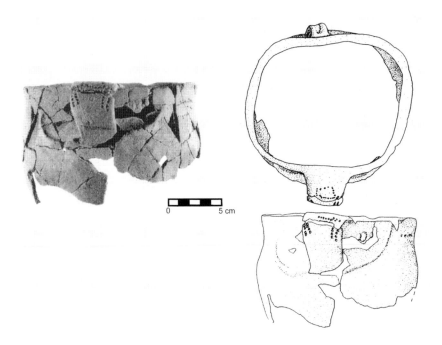

13 Square-mouthed vessel from feature 71 (grave?) at Escolives-Sainte-Camille

non-Italian examples reflect local manufacture in technology as well as decoration, it has been suggested that square-mouthed pottery should be considered as a phenomenon of imitation, perhaps related to the circulation of the Alpine eclogite axes. It has also been suggested that square-mouthed vessels may represent clay replicas of wooden bowls, impressions of which have apparently been found at Erdeven (Cassen *et al.* 2000).

Some of the Cerny square-mouthed pots are decorated with an applied ribbon in the curious shape of a 'moustache' extending from the handle to the upper part of the vessel (*13*). Such decoration is known on other pottery of the Cerny horizon across northern France and its iconographic symbolism, however stylised, has clear meaning against the background of the importance of cattle. Indeed, the association of bovine symbolism with an exotic origin of the vessel form may further emphasise their exceptional function: they could have been destined for serving certain specific foods (sometimes served in wooden bowls?) – foods which were also considered suitable either for consumption at funerary feasts or as provision for the dead.

Flint, stone and other industries

Flint and crystalline rocks were also the principal raw materials for the manufacture of tools used by the Cerny communities. Some materials moved long distances. Some of the polished flint axes in Brittany are made from flint mined at Bretteville-le-Rabet in Normandy, while the pale axes made from the so-called 'Douhet' flint most probably derive from the Charente region. Exotic materials such as jasper and opal from the Loire are also found in Breton tombs (Desloges 1986; Le Roux 1999).

Indeed, Brittany became one of the final destinations in the distribution of the highly prestigious jade axes manufactured in the north Alpine region. These exquisitely made and heavily polished axes were never used as tools but played an important role in the creation and maintenance of social elites. Many were subsequently disposed of in hoards or provided, in combination with other exotica such as stone bracelets, as goods to accompany the dead. The chronology of these axes needs refining, as they seem to have been circulated throughout the whole of the middle Neolithic, but such exchanges – highlighting the Paris Basin as one of the major communication routes – began during the Cerny culture (Pétrequin *et al.* 1997).

The exploitation of Breton dolerite rocks for the manufacture of polished stone axes – especially at the famous Plussulien axe factory – may well have begun at the time of the Cerny culture, but the mass extraction and manufacture of these axes, encountered as far as the Pyrenees and Alsace, must on present evidence date to the later period from the end of the fifth and beginning of the fourth millennium BC (Le Roux 1999).

Everyday tools, however, were for the most part made from locally available materials. Cerny tools from the south Paris Basin, studied by Augereau, were made almost exclusively from locally available flint. The technology was based predominantly on flakes, with very few blade tools. Indeed, as already noted, the lack of blade tools has been related directly to a lesser interest in cereal growing in this region. Two types of tool are worth highlighting: the flake axes and arrowheads. We have already noted the importance of hunting in this area, and the profusion of transverse arrowheads – with flat retouch in the south Paris Basin, and different retouches in the neighbouring areas – may indicate the need for affirmation of regional ethnic identities.

Polished flint axes are not generally encountered in the Cerny of the south Paris Basin: the local flint sources are not suitable for such large tools and it is not clear whether there were difficulties in obtaining them from elsewhere. Instead that function seems to have been fulfilled by a new tool in the form of a much smaller but equally efficient flake axe (*le tranchet*; Augereau 1993). Naturally, as their widespread use in the TRB culture testifies, flake axes are used for many activities but they are particularly suitable for dealing with relatively light, secondary vegetation growth of the sort associated with intensive pastoral activities.

Other items were made of organic materials, although in many cases there is only circumstantial evidence for this. Animal bones were used both for extraordinary items which we find in graves and for utilitarian tools. The T-shaped axes, which may have worked as well as flake axes, continued to be made from antler. Animal bones were fashioned into heavy tools such as picks, as well as delicate implements such as scrapers, perforators or needles. Bones and teeth, especially from wild species, were fashioned into beads and pendants (Sidéra 2000).

SUMMARY

In comparison with other regions, the emergence of the Neolithic in north-west Europe must be understood as a complex process. In purely economic terms the standard cultivated plants and domesticated animals did eventually, as in other areas, form the backbone of north-western economies. The uniqueness of the process of neolithisation lies in the active participation of the indigenous hunter-gatherers, who modified and transformed the standard elements of the Danubian 'Neolithic package' in response to their own economic, social and ideological requirements. While these new agricultural practices began to change the natural environment of north-west Europe, the most powerful and original manifestation of these developments was the creation of a rich ceremonial landscape. In contrast to the rather diffuse nature of the settlement, the ritual landscape created permanent and dramatic settings for social interaction, expression of beliefs and burial practices. Among the most dramatic and tangible remains of that landscape are the first monumental cemeteries which form the subject of the later part of this book.

CHAPTER 3

MESOLITHIC AND DANUBIAN BURIAL TRADITIONS

INTRODUCTORY THEORETICAL CONCEPTS

For well over a century archaeologists have been keenly interested in the interpretation of prehistoric burial ritual. In the later nineteenth century, inspiration from anthropological and sociological disciplines focused attention on the importance of religious beliefs, particularly belief in an afterlife and worship of ancestors. Sir John Lubbock, applying some of these ideas to his interpretation of prehistory, recognised that the treatment of the dead differed in respect to the age, sex and social standing of individuals; moreover, he believed that there was a direct relationship between grave goods and belief in the afterlife (Lubbock 1870).

An important set of concepts, subsequently applied in archaeology, were the ideas of the early twentieth-century French sociologists who looked at religious phenomena – burial included – in the context of social systems; ideas which subsequently inspired many ethnographic and anthropological studies. Hertz, for example, thought the belief in the afterlife expressed the friction between the transitory nature of the individual's life and the endurance of the society's structure. Van Gennep's work offered an important concept of *rites de passage* – the stages of separation, transition and incorporation – in the analysis of burial practices, particularly the symbolic isolation of the body in the cemetery, an area geographically and conceptually different from that of the living. Finally, Durkheim's general concept of sacred and profane, as well as his affirmation of the importance of 'social facts' in all explanations of human behaviour, became key concepts in the anthropology and archaeology of death (Carr 1995).

From the late 1960s until the mid-1980s, social structure and social organisation featured prominently within archaeological burial research, albeit within a very narrow approach. The processual paradigm, with its materialist-ecological perspective, did not regard religious beliefs as significant in cultural practices. Binford's ethnographic cross-cultural survey of burial practices concluded that the variations observed in burial were directly related to the form and organisation of social systems, and that archaeologists should study the social structure rather than the form of burials (Binford 1971). The alternative, that religious beliefs might have an important influence on the differences in burial practices, was simply not considered.

Binford's work inspired many archaeologists, in America and in Europe, to develop models for the interpretation of burial practices as a prism through which to view the social organisation of past communities. Among the more influential were, firstly, Saxe's hypothesis that corporate, lineal descent groups which used and controlled critical and restricted resources also developed formal areas devoted exclusively to the disposal of the dead, i.e. cemeteries; and, secondly, Tainter's argument that social ranking of individuals was expressed through the amount of energy expended in funeral activities. Interestingly, Tainter did not find that the quantity and quality of grave goods were strongly related to the rank of the deceased (Saxe 1970, Tainter 1978).

In Britain, Renfrew developed ideas about megaliths as symbolic expressions of territorial behaviour practised by small segmentary societies, which he applied to his studies of the British as well as the continental megaliths (Renfrew 1972, 1973, 1976). The relationships between social organisation and burial practices were further explored in a variety of archaeological contexts and *The archaeology of death* (Chapman *et al.* 1981) is probably a classic example of this genre.

The processual approaches were influential in the field of burial theory and they also highlighted the potential richness of the archaeological burial record. However, the emphasis on social relationships, as displayed through burials, ignored the fact that symbolic and ideological values could also be represented in funerary practices, and that an understanding of the interaction between social organisation and beliefs was necessary if past burial practices were to be fully interpreted.

Thus, from the late 1980s onwards, ideological and religious concepts became once again important in the study of burial practices. Hodder's main tenet that culture is 'meaningfully constituted' is important: it suggests that as in all other activities, so in burial practice, the individuals in a community will play an active role in the rituals. Ambiguity of beliefs and symbols could be used during funerals to express individuals' motivations as well as the society's world views, rather than merely to fossilise the community's social organisation (Hodder 1982). Indeed, the way burials are placed, in relation to the living areas and within the natural landscape at large, is important to an understanding of the funerary ritual in its wider setting (Tilley 1994, 1999).

Some of these basic theoretical concepts will be explored later in this chapter as well as in the chapter dealing with the interpretation of monumental cemeteries. We should now review the Mesolithic and Danubian burial practices. While this brief panoramic sketch does not permit detailed consideration of the extraordinary wealth of evidence available, we shall consider some important general issues which, subsequently, will aid our understanding of the dramatic funerary practices which emerged in the TRB and the Cerny cultures.

Mesolithic and Danubian burials have been known in north-west Europe since the nineteenth century, for example from the famous Danish shell-midden at Ertebølle or from the Hinkelstein cemetery in Rhine-Hessen. Danubian cemeteries continued to be discovered throughout the twentieth century, from Flomborn (excavated between 1903 and 1905) to the spectacular necropoli at Nitra in Slovakia, Elsloo in the Netherlands, Niedermerz in Lower Rhineland and the numerous Bavarian cemeteries excavated from the 1960s to the 1980s. Mesolithic cemeteries were also being investigated from the 1930s onwards, for example at Téviec and Hoëdic on the Atlantic coast and at Oleni'ostrov in the East Baltic region.

However, until recently, the specific subject of Mesolithic and Danubian burial practices did not feature prominently in research. Scholars of the Mesolithic were more concerned with creating complex regional typologies of lithic industries, and with the economic and ecological adaptations of late hunter-gatherers to the different environments they inhabited. Similarly, the extraordinarily rich corpus of evidence, of more than 50 cemeteries and over 2,500 *Linearbandkeramik* graves across Europe – and this does not include the later Danubian evidence which is yet to become the subject of an overall synthesis – has until recently received little attention (Jeunesse 1997). Once again, the reasons are deeply rooted in research traditions in which novel economic resources in the form of cereals and domesticated animals, as well as settlements with their spectacular house remains and vast amounts of decorated pottery, have attracted all the attention. Moreover, since Pavúk's (1972) interpretation of the burials from the Nitra cemetery, Slovakia, in which he evoked a picture of a largely egalitarian society, there was little interest in the social or ritual aspects of Danubian burials.

MESOLITHIC BURIALS IN NORTH-WEST EUROPE

The discovery, in the mid-1970s, of a group of 18 graves in the area of Bøgebakken at the Vedbæk Fjord on the north east coast of Zealand, was a turning point in Mesolithic funerary research (Albrethsen and Brinch Petersen 1977). Not only did the experience gained at Vedbæk lead to the application of new excavation strategies on other Mesolithic sites in Scandinavia, contributing to a massive increase in burial data, but, significantly, it also provided a new conceptual direction in the interpretation of Mesolithic burial practices.

Since then many burials have been discovered in the process of excavation of Mesolithic sites. The wealth of evidence deriving from the recent Scandinavian investigations – for example further localities around the Vedbæk Fjord; the two Skateholm cemeteries in Scania (where not only people but also dogs were buried), the more recently encountered burials at Tågerup, Scania; the shell-midden at Nederst on East Zealand; as well as discoveries from submerged sites such as at Møllegabet on Dejrø or at Tybrind Vig off Fyn – is so rich that it will continue to exercise many future generations of researchers (Kannegaard Nielsen and Brinch Petersen 1993; Larsson 1988a, 1988b, 1989a, 1989b, 1990, 1995, 1999; Malm 1995; Skaarup 1995a, 1995b). However, discoveries elsewhere in north-west Europe are equally important. No Mesolithic burials were known from the Paris Basin before 1990, but now at least four sites demonstrate the variety of burial customs; other recent discoveries in western France, in Belgium and in Poland further underline the diversity of Mesolithic burial practices.

The dead during the Mesolithic were inhumed and cremated, and each practice involved a bewildering variety of ways in which it could be performed. Primary inhumation was by far the commonest and was practised throughout the period although, interestingly, Mesolithic burials also provide evidence of secondary interment and of repeated manipulation of human remains. Thus the site of La Chaussée-Tirancourt '*Le Petit Marais*' offers a rare example of a secondary burial – a pit with a bundle of long bones and a skull placed on top of them – while at two Belgian sites (at the rock shelter of Autours and in the cave of Margaux) multiple human remains were subject to deliberate displacement, rearrangements and extractions over a considerable period of time (Ducrocq 1999; Cauwe 2001). Indeed, the extraction and manipulation of fragments of human bodies has also been documented in the context of the so-called primary interments: extra body fragments have been encountered in graves at the Breton shell-middens, several skeletons from Skateholm had parts of extremities removed, and some empty graves give a clear impression of bodies having been exhumed soon after the burial. Moreover, perforated human teeth were sometimes incorporated into jewellery – as is well illustrated by an ornament on one of the bodies at Bøgebakken.

Primary inhumations may be single, double or multiple; six individuals were buried in grave K at Téviec and eight at Strøby Egede on eastern Zealand although generally the numbers are smaller. Most of the dead were laid out extended on the back: this was commonly practised in southern Scandinavia, as is demonstrated by many graves at the cemeteries at Skateholm I and II and at Vedbæk. Equally, this manner of burial is encountered outwith northern Europe, as was the case with the first individual placed in the communal grave pit at Varennes (Val-de-Reuil, Eure; Billard *et al.* 2001). Seated burials, while not frequent, are known from the earlier cemetery at Skateholm, from a few graves at Téviec and Hoëdic (*colour plate 6*), from Auneau (Eure; Verjux 1999a) and from Poland; the famous Janisławice grave has been known in literature for a long time and, more recently, one of the Mszano graves has been interpreted as an example of a seated burial (Marciniak 1993). Influences from the Danubian sphere may very well have led to the adoption, during the late Mesolithic, of a flexed manner of burial – such as was common on the Breton shell-middens and was also practised during the time when Skateholm I cemetery was used, where up to two-fifths of the dead were placed in a variety of crouched positions (Larsson 1989a, 221).

Fragments of burned human bones have been anecdotal on many sites, and recent discoveries have confirmed cremation as another form of Mesolithic burial. To the example known for quite some time from Oirschot, Netherlands (Arts and Hoogland 1987), others can now be added. At La Chaussée-Tirancourt '*Le Petit Marais*', remains of several cremated individuals, collected from the funerary pyre together with their burnt shell jewellery, were placed in another pit (Ducrocq and Ketterer 1995, 253). A few cremations have been recorded at Skateholm and cremation deposits have also been discovered in the locality called Gøngehusvej 7, in the Vedbæk Fjord (Brinch Petersen and Meiklejohn 2003). One pit (N) contained a mixture of cremated remains of five individuals. Some of their bones were gathered from the funerary pyre together with oak charcoal, burnt flint blades and animal teeth pendants, and arranged in the pit with long bones next to and on top of others. In another pit (Æ) burned bones of a young adult were placed on top of a wooden tray and then covered with the body of a three-month-old roe deer; according to the excavators this is the only Mesolithic burial for which a seasonal date at the beginning of September can be offered (*ibid.* 489).

Grave structures

Many of the graves were made simply by digging a pit of an appropriate size directly into the ground, but others were clearly more elaborate. Small stone-lined chambers had been constructed in the shell-middens at Téviec and Hoëdic: some were sealed with flat capstones, offering suitable arrangements for subsequent interments (*14*). The placement of red deer antlers in a framework around the body, known from Hoëdic, Skateholm and La Vergne, may be all that is left from some sort of protective construction of animal skins or other organic materials; indeed, at La Vergne auroch horns may have been employed in a similar fashion (Duday and Courtaud 1998; Courtaud *et al.* 1999). The positioning of antlers under the shoulders and hips of the deceased, as observed at Bøgebakken, may indicate remains of a funerary bier placed at the bottom of a grave pit.

The seated burials, by virtue of their complex position, would have required special arrangements. The young man buried at Auneau had 300kg of stones placed on the lower body to help prop him up, the antlers in the grave XV at Skateholm II may have performed a similar function, and at Mszano the grave

14 Double burial in
grave A at Téviec.
Péquart, M. et al. 1937

pit was dug on two levels to facilitate the seated position, although unfortunately no bones have survived.

Timber linings of graves can be inferred from some very regular pits and
there are also examples of timber structures projecting above the surface, having
been set on fire at the end of the burial ceremony (Mszano and Skateholm). In
addition, from southern Scandinavia there are many examples of dugout canoes
providing a final resting place, either weighed by stones and moored under the
shallows, or placed inland within the grave pit (Skaarup 1995a).

Burial rituals

Some of the burials undoubtedly were very simple affairs; the dead are not
equipped with anything and if funerary ceremonies were performed they left
no trace in the archaeological record. Others are not only richly endowed with
grave goods but appear to have been subject to elaborate funerary rituals.
Remains of several structures found next to graves at Skateholm suggest that,
prior to the burial, the dead may have been laid out in mortuaries where
dressing of the corpses, sprinkling with ochre and other preparations took
place. Structures near burials have been found elsewhere – for example, on
several sites at the Vedbæk Fjord and at Mszano – but their interpretation
revolves around the nature of the sites: are these normal settlements with burials
interspersed among the houses of the living, or are they locations devoted
exclusively to attending to and caring for the dead?

On the analysis of the stomach contents from several well-preserved bodies at Skateholm, Larsson has argued that the dying were given a 'last supper' consisting of a fish-based meal. While such remains undoubtedly constitute the very last meal consumed before death, the concept of a 'last supper' implies the anticipation of death. There may indeed have been cultural or religious requirements on the feeding of the seriously ill, the injured or the very old, but many must have died unexpectedly. Some appear to have died of wounds received in skirmishes, and the evidence of burials of young women accompanied by newborn children in numerous Scandinavian burials suggests that many died in or soon after childbirth.

Burial ceremonies frequently involved some sort of feasting by the living. Hearths, some with food traces, are associated with graves on many sites. At Mszano about a dozen hearths with food remains were set in a circle in the vicinity of the graves, and one of them contained a complete burnt adult wild boar and a piglet. Stone-built hearths crowned the graves at Téviec and similar, if less substantial, traces of funerary fires were observed at Hoëdic. These fires, in contrast to the 'domestic' hearths of the middens, did not burn fiercely and it is not clear whether food was cooked on them. The mandibles of wild boar and of red deer found in them were placed after the fires were extinguished and thus may represent token remains from feast food cooked elsewhere on the site, with the principal role of the fires as purificatory and sealing acts. Several graves at Skateholm had hearths either above or within the partly filled-in grave pit; this involved not only human but dog burials as well.

There are other interesting aspects observed in relation to food. The fact that food, in organic containers, was placed in Mesolithic graves demonstrates that the tradition of food offerings for the dead began long before the adoption of farming. Skateholm offers evidence for organic receptacles with food being placed in the graves, and this must have been practised elsewhere. The possibly Mesolithic burial pit (no. 5) under the Erdeven long barrow in Brittany, revealed an imprint of a rectangular wooden (?) vessel placed in it (Cassen *et al.* 2000, 53, 423) and food may well have been placed on funerary pyres: burnt fish bones were apparently found with the cremations at Gøngehusvej 7 (Strassburg 2000, 169).

The types of food placed in the graves and consumed during the ceremonies at Skateholm provide a fascinating new dimension: the food in the graves is mostly fish. At least eight individuals had fish provisions placed in their graves and several others had fish incorporated in the grave fills. On the other hand, food traces from the activity areas around the graves reveal that, apart from fish, wild pig, red and roe deer were eaten. In the absence of final reports, and against the background of different interpretations of the function of Skateholm sites (permanent settlement, temporary camp, a special locality for the marginalised members of the Mesolithic community), it is difficult to offer an interpretation. Larsson has argued that fish consumption, while not surprising on a

15 Ceremonial pile of animal skulls over the grave at Varennes. *Cauwe 2001*

sea lagoon, was also symbolically important as representative of the spiritual underworld and thus played an important role in funerary rituals. Indeed, the scanty evidence of fish consumption among the early Scandinavian farmers has been argued to reflect a dramatic change in the cosmology rather than a new dietary fashion. On the other hand, one could also argue that, while the dead were indeed provided with 'spiritually significant food', the living used the burial ceremony as an opportunity to feast and did so by eating the rare and luxurious hunted meats.

Recently, an extraordinary discovery at Varennes (*15*; Billard *et al.* 2001) has further increased the spectrum of the animal funerary symbolism. Here a grave pit, which received human remains on at least two separate occasions, was surmounted by a massive pile of wild animal skulls. A huge cattle skull with horns still attached was placed over the centre of the grave and surrounded by numerous red and roe deer skulls with antlers; this pyramid rested upon the long bones – wild pig and beaver were also identified – and the whole arrangement was set on fire. The excavators have compared this to examples of structures burnt over Mesolithic graves, but a different interpretation is equally plausible. These large and dangerous animals were not easy to hunt; much has been written on the subject of social prestige derived from prowess in hunting, and foods thus obtained may have been reserved for rare and special occasions. Funerals would have provided at least one such context, as much for the consumption of prestigious food as for an affirmation of the social significance of hunting. The remains of ungulates in foods recovered in the vicinity of graves support such an interpretation. The ritual at Varennes may thus relate to a massive funerary feast, with the leftovers sacrificed in commemoration of the spirits of the animals and of the dead placed in the pit below.

Jewellery and tools, as well as other items, played a role in funerary rituals, although there are interesting regional variations. We have already alluded to the differences in personal adornments among the various Mesolithic communities. Thus, across the North European Plain and in southern Scandinavia, jewellery made from wild animal teeth was paramount, although occasionally shells had been used. This took the form of necklaces, waist and hip belts and head gear. Perforated red deer teeth, sometimes accounting for 30 animals within a single ornament, were most common but those from wild pig, seal, elk, auroch and, indeed, human teeth, had also been used. Pectorals of animal bones – with or without perforated animal teeth – were sometimes worn on the chest, and the presence of bone pins near the head suggests either elaborate hair arrangements or caps decorated with teeth, hooves etc.

While such jewellery was undoubtedly decorative and indicative of the social status of the wearer, many scholars argue that it also played an important symbolic role – with bodily orifices considered as dangerous places in need of protection, in life as much as in death, by means of correctly composed ornaments (Tilley 1996, 66). Indeed, it was precisely these parts of the body, the head, thoracic region and hips that were regularly coloured with red ochre.

In the west of Europe, the same protective body practices seem to have relied upon marine shells, with only a sporadic inclusion of wild boar and red deer teeth. The dead at Téviec and Hoëdic (*colour plate 6*) were placed in their graves with necklaces, armbands and hairnets made, by and large, of two types of shell: the cowrie shell (*Trivia europea*) and the periwinkle (*Littorina obtusata*). It has been demonstrated long ago that male jewellery contained a greater proportion of cowrie shells, while that of women used more periwinkles (Taborin 1974). Shell ornaments, however, were also important further inland: the cremated bones from La Chaussée-Tirancourt 'Le Petit Marais' had been gathered from the pyre together with the remains of shell beads, and the burials from La Vergne, Charente-Maritime (Courtaud *et al.* 1999, 289) had ornaments of dog whelk (*Hinia reticulata*) and tusk shell (*Dentalium*).

Tools made of flint, bone and stone were placed in many graves. Flint blades and knives as well as arrows tipped with transverse points are common everywhere. In the north, core flint axes as well as the imported Danubian *Schuhleistenkeile* were placed in some graves. An important category of grave goods are tools made of organic materials – bone points and bone daggers, and axes and hammers made of antler.

There is no scope here to discuss all the implications of the grave goods and rituals associated with the Mesolithic burials and, indeed, such discussions have been plentiful elsewhere. However, the Mesolithic evidence has taught us renewed caution in the use of stereotypes we have become accustomed to: women could be, and were, buried with typically 'male' accessories such as bone knives, blades or arrows. And how would we have interpreted the dog graves from Skateholm had their skeletons not survived?

Evidence brought to light in the past two decades has shown very clearly that Mesolithic burial practices were not only about fossilising the social order of the living. Larsson and others have stressed that the complexity of burial ritual at Scandinavian cemeteries – and this can be extended to Mesolithic burial elsewhere – went beyond the mere social parameters, and that it encompassed the entire cosmology of the hunter-gatherer world: the relationships between humans, animals, the land and the entire supernatural world as they understood it.

DANUBIAN BURIALS

At first sight, the Danubian funerary practices appear as a complete contrast to the Mesolithic burial traditions. The dead were buried in cemeteries which were clearly separated from settlements; crouched inhumations in simple pits (*16*) were accompanied by a stereotypical set of grave goods which included pottery, sometimes stone and flint tools, and a set of ornaments made from spondylus shells. There was little difference in the treatment of individuals; children were hardly ever present but, in some cemeteries, older men's graves stood out from the rest by virtue of a richer assortment of tools, usually including stone axes and more jewellery. Such was the traditional view of the Danubian funerary practices that went hand in hand with the idea of the homogeneity of the Danubian world in most of its other aspects. This picture is altering dramatically and, while not so explicitly publicised in the English literature, our understanding of the Danubian funerary practices is undergoing a major revolution akin to that which has shaken our views of the Mesolithic burials.

The Danubian dead were buried in many different locations, although cemeteries were, indeed, in use from the very beginning of the *Linearbandkeramik*, as is clearly shown at Vedrovice in Slovakia (Podborský *et al.* 2002) with the first

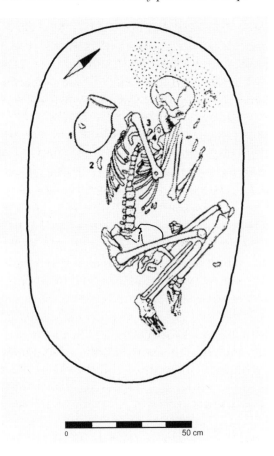

0   50 cm

16 Early Danubian burial at
Vedrovice. *Podborský* et al. *2002*

burials belonging to the Ib local phase. While cemeteries were typical of both early and later Danubian groups, the vagaries of research mean that the greatest concentrations are known in the Rhine and Danube river valleys, while other areas are less well represented. They vary in size considerably: some are relatively small, for example 37 graves at Ensisheim and 22 at Mulhouse-Est (previously known in the literature as Rixheim) in Alsace, while others are quite large, for example 228 burials at Aiterhofen in Bavaria or 311 graves at Wandersleben in Thuringia (Jeunesse 1996a, 1996b). The graves must have been clearly marked on the surface since, even in the most densely used cemeteries, they do not as a rule overlap. Indeed the clusters of graves within cemeteries, which may have accrued over several generations and which are usually interpreted as representing family or lineage groups, suggest that knowledge about the dead was transmitted orally and it was known who had been buried where. However, not all settlements had a cemetery: in spite of great efforts none has ever been found around the multi-period settlement of Bylany in Bohemia; Niedermerz, on the Aldenhovener Platte, cannot be specifically associated with any of the settlements excavated along the Merzbach river; and, so far, there are no cemeteries in the Paris Basin (Jeunesse 1997).

Apart from cemeteries, burials were regularly placed within the settlements. We find them associated with the houses (usually near the walls or in the lateral pits), in silos and other types of pit as well as in deliberately dug grave pits, sometimes in little clusters. These arrangements, curiously, seem to evoke the hunter-gatherer practices discussed earlier of placing their dead among the living. This manner of burial is found everywhere, even on sites that had a cemetery in the vicinity, and therefore it should not be regarded as a subsidiary practice; in fact it forces us to reconsider our image of the Danubian village (chapter 6). Thus at Vedrovice, where two cemeteries about 500m apart were in use, at least 12 graves were found on the settlement, with the 9 children buried in the lateral house pits (Podborský *et al.* 2002, 12). In the Paris Basin all graves are found in settlements: this is valid as much for the *Linearbandkeramik* as for the subsequent Villeneuve-Saint-Germain culture (Jeunesse 1997; Veit 1992).

While, on account of the acidic soil conditions, no burials have ever been found at Bylany, there are finds indicating that some of the settlement pits here did contain burials. Indeed, disused houses may have served as burial places; during the LBK they were not built over by new houses but rather left to become ruins. Ulrich Veit mentions an old find from Zauschwitz, where the house seems to have been burnt after the burial of a child (1992, 118), and a recent report of a burial inside a long house from the region of Baden-Württemberg, where a substantial number of graves have been found in disused domestic contexts (Orschiedt 1997), supports this idea. When parts of a settlement became abandoned they provided equally suitable burial places: at Vaihingen, in Baden-Württemberg, the partly silted-up ditch became a burial ground to about fifty dead and so were the disused lateral house pits in its vicinity (Krause 1997). Several graves, among them a multiple grave of seven children, were found in the ditch at Menneville in the Paris Basin (Farruggia *et al.* 1996).

On the northern periphery of the Danubian world, the Lengyel Brześć Kujawski group provides equally interesting examples of such a practice, with regular placement of the dead in between the trapezoidal houses which are typical of this period. At the Brześć Kujawski settlement itself the graves appear to have been intimately associated with the houses. The inhabitants of house number 56, for example, were buried just a few metres to the west of their dwelling – three males and six females, all of a fairly advanced age (average 40-45) – their trade as specialists in the working of antler, bone and shell-beads well documented in the yard of the house and reflected in their grave goods (Grygiel 1986).

The graves themselves were simple pits, oval in shape and hardly larger than was necessary to accommodate a crouched inhumation. There is little evidence of any constructions within the grave pits themselves. Examples of post-hole arrangements at the edges of the grave have been found, for example at Sondershausen and at Mulhouse-Est (Jeunesse 1997, 60, Fig. 16), suggesting some sort of wooden construction, but these are very rare.

The typical Danubian burial ritual was relatively formal: single individuals were placed in a crouched position, lying on their left side with arms crossed in front of the face, oriented from east to west, with head to the east. Some scholars have argued that these orientations reflect beliefs associated with the importance of heavenly bodies, with the setting sun symbolically providing a gateway to the other world (see Podborský *et al.* 2002 for astro-archaeological analysis of the orientations at Vedrovice). However, nearly every cemetery shows deviations from this classic placement. Some of the dead may be oriented differently, laid on the right, with different arm and leg positions; in the later period women tended to be buried on their left side and men on their right. Moreover, in the later Danubian cemeteries, extended inhumations were not uncommon; such was the case with all the burials discovered at Trebur in Hessen (Spatz 1997), and a number of scholars have argued that the use of extended inhumation by some Danubian groups is one of the examples of influence from the local hunter-gatherer communities.

Cremation, while not common, was practised concurrently with inhumation. The best example comes from the Dutch cemetery at Elsloo, where over 40 per cent of the dead were cremated, it is also known from a number of Bavarian cemeteries, and a double rite was noted also at Miskovice in Bohemia. However, there are no regional rules: at Niedermerz, which is only 40km from the contemporary and similar-sized cemetery at Elsloo, only 9 per cent of the dead were cremated (Jeunesse 1997; Zápotocká 1998a).

In contrast to the preceding and subsequent periods, there is little evidence that Danubian practices included secondary burial, but occasionally human remains were subject to manipulation after the burial. At Ensisheim and at Vaihingen several graves show rearrangement of the bones, for example moving skulls into different positions. Discovery of isolated human bones on settlements should be treated with caution – they may indicate circulation of ancestral remains but, equally, they may derive from accidental disturbances of settlement burials.

Grave goods

As in the Mesolithic, the use of ochre was important and nearly all the Danubian graves reveal evidence of this substance. It was used in a similar fashion: either sprinkled all over the body or concentrated around the head and/or hip area. Lumps of ochre were sometimes incorporated into jewellery. The presence of grinding stones with traces of dyes – ochre or graphite – suggests that dyes were used regularly. They were, of course, used to paint pottery (the most attractive painted ceramics come from the Lengyel tradition of the so-called Moravian Painted Ware) but equally they may have been used in body decoration. Indeed, discoveries of fragments of painted figurines in central and southern Germany suggest that body decoration with paint may have been practised (*17*), although it is impossible to say whether this was a requirement of the burial ritual or whether such decoration was also commonly applied in life.

Pottery – most often decorated – was placed in the graves but not with everyone; at Vedrovice, for instance, only just over half of the individuals (54.2 per cent) had pottery, and graves without pots are found everywhere. When present, there are usually one or two pots but sometimes more: an elderly male in grave 69 at Vedrovice had four complete vessels (plus sherds of another) and similar quantities are known from a number of graves at other cemeteries (Jeunesse 1997, 70). We have already noted the importance of food for the dead in the Mesolithic, where it was placed in the graves in organic containers. If the Danubian dead were also provided with food, could different pots reflect different types of food, and did the bowls contain one sort and amphorae another? Was it perhaps a mark of distinction to be provided with several different dishes for the journey beyond and did the number of pots reflect this?

These questions cannot, of course, be answered without analyses of food content from the graves, but there are indications, within later Danubian contexts, that food might have been one of the criteria of social differences. Spectacular finds, in the form of entire animal carcasses or substantial joints of meat, have been made in some of the graves at Trebur (Spatz 1997). Such practices are infrequent during the LBK – although we may quote an example of a richly equipped elderly man from Aiterhofen (grave no.102) who was provided with a joint of pork – but have been noted on a number of other later Danubian sites along the Rhine, in the Paris Basin and in Bavaria. At Trebur, the pork joints seem to have been reserved for men while women were given mutton, the joints being variously placed by the head, on the upper part of the body or covering the legs. Quite apart from the possible implications of such gifts in terms of social distinctions, the use of domestic species as food offerings provides a significant contrast to the use of wild animals in the sphere of

17 Tentative reconstruction of late Danubian body decoration, based on patterns from clay statuettes found in south Germany. *Behrends 1997*

personal adornment (see below) as it underlines a complex attitude on the part of the later Danubian communities towards the wild and the domesticated parts of their world.

Among the tools, flint blades, arrows, grinding stones (sometimes used for grinding various dyes), axes and hammer stones are commonly found. The finds of arrowheads are important, indicating that the Danubians frequently used bows and arrows and that they did so from the very beginning, as several of the Vedrovice graves have yielded fine trapezoidal arrowheads; at Schwetzingen the discovery of numerous arrowheads, grouped in the vicinity of the head or shoulder, suggests that the dead had quivers slung over their shoulder (Behrends 1997, 19).

Jewellery

The Danubians appear to have been just as fond of jewellery as the hunter-gatherers, and the dead frequently carried it to their graves. Marine and fresh-water shells, marble, hard rock (schist) and, later, animal bones and teeth, were used. Spondylus (*Spondylus gaedoropus*) was, of course, the raw material par excellence, used in the manufacture of various beads, bracelets, medallions and belt-hooks (*colour plate* 7). The finds from the LBK cemeteries suggest that this material, originating in the wide Mediterranean zone, was acquired in considerable quantities and it evidently had not just ornamental but religious and magical properties; broken pieces were not thrown away but reused. Marble was also fashioned into beads, as seen in grave 9/88 at Vedrovice, where a young

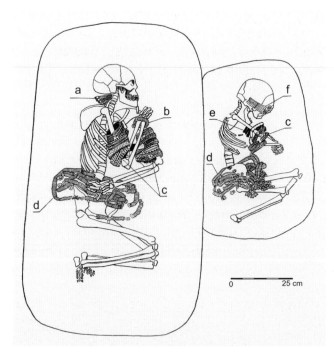

18 Burials of a female and a child from Krusza Zamkowa, Kujavia: a) copper bead earrings; b) shell bracelet; c) engraved bone armbands; d) shell

woman (18-20 years of age) was buried not only with an armband and a medallion of Spondylus, but also with necklaces and bracelets made of over 500 tubular marble beads, as well as additional items made of shells of *Lithoglyphus naticoides* (*colour plate 8;* Podborský *et al.* 2002, 110-115, Figs 116-117).

While the presence of jewellery made from wild animal teeth is rare in the LBK, the later Danubian communities developed a real craze for such ornaments, particularly deer teeth and wild boars' tusks. This represents a major innovation and must indicate an ideological change sufficiently important to be displayed in the funerary customs. Later Danubian graves from Alsace show that wild boars' tusks were used to make bracelets, replacing the earlier ones made of shells; deer teeth, as well as those of smaller carnivores, notably fox, also make an appearance. Some women at Trebur have jewellery made of many deer teeth; apparently 115 deer had to be killed to provide the woman in grave no.63 with the 230 teeth used in her ornaments (Spatz 1997, 167).

Interesting regional variations are provided by the late Danubian communities in the area of Kujavia, where the Brześć Kujawski group dead were buried according to specific rituals. The men were buried on their right side and frequently accompanied by bone points and T-shaped antler axes. The women were placed on their left side and wore ostentatious jewellery: necklaces made of wild animal teeth (deer, wild boar, dog and wolf) and dozens of engraved armbands shaped from animal ribs. Ornaments were also made of shells and, significantly, of copper. At Krusza Zamkowa, for example, an adult woman was buried with earrings made of 97 copper beads, 18 decorated armbands and a four-strand hip belt of 2,295 shell beads; a child, five to six years old, had a head diadem of two spectacle copper spirals, 181 copper and 66 shell beads, a necklace of six copper sheets and a six-strand hip belt of 2,095 shell beads (*18;* Bednarczyk *et al.* 1980). Equally elaborate jewellery, including headdresses of copper strips, was found with the dead at Osłonki (Bogucki 2003).

EMERGENCE OF CEMETERIES: CONCEPTS AND INTERPRETATIONS

Having briefly reviewed the Mesolithic and Danubian burial practices, we should now devote some consideration to the question of cemeteries. While the study of prehistoric burial practices has, in large measure, relied upon ethnographic evidence – most strongly within the processual paradigm – the emergence of cemeteries in Europe during the sixth millennium BC is not an issue that can benefit from ethnographic parallels, since there are no records reaching that far back; we need to rely directly on the archaeological evidence itself.

A cemetery is an area dedicated exclusively to the interment of the dead; whether it is in a cave, in an open space, close by or at a distance from a settlement is not really so significant; it is, however, important that, once chosen, the area continues to be used for repeated burials – that is what makes it a cemetery.

If we accept this definition, then there can be little doubt that the Danubians buried some of their dead in cemeteries – locations distinct in space and in function from the settlements, and used over a sufficiently long period of time to be considered as such. Sites with numerous Mesolithic burials are referred to in the literature as cemeteries (Hoëdic and Téviec in Brittany, Vedbæk in Denmark and Skateholm in Sweden), but not everyone agrees with such an interpretation (Kannegaard Nielsen and Brinch Petersen 1993; Meiklejohn *et al.* 1998). Indeed, with the possible exception of some of the eastern Baltic sites (Oleni'ostrov and Zvejnieki; Jacobs 1995; Gerhards *et al.* 2003), the known Mesolithic 'cemetery' sites from north-west Europe are not reserved exclusively for burial.

The graves, even if concentrated in groups, appear within the settled areas; every site excavated at Vedbæk yielded burials, sometimes in association with hut structures as at Gøngehusvej no.7, or interspersed with settlement layers. Similar conditions seem to have been present at the Skateholm sites, and the preliminary studies suggest that groupings of graves here may involve related individuals. While the stratigraphy from some sites may be ambiguous, burials from shell-middens equally imply that there was little separation of the dead from the living.

Thus, on the one hand, the groups of Mesolithic graves located within settlements suggest that the living spaces were not segregated from the spaces for the dead and that '...people were clearly living between and on top of their recently deceased' (Meiklejohn *et al.* 1998, 205). At the same time, it is clear that the locations of graves were well known over several generations and respected. On the Scandinavian sites there is hardly any overlap between the graves, even if they are found in close proximity to one another, and it is generally assumed that they were marked in some manner on the surface. Elsewhere, at Téviec and Hoëdic, the graves must also have been marked, since some of them were reopened to admit additional burials.

While it is important to bear in mind that cemeteries may have appeared for a variety of reasons, perhaps this is one of the scenarios which could be evoked to explain their emergence. That is how some of them came into being – initially as areas within the settlements which, while not physically apart, had over a period of time accumulated a number of graves. In consequence of such an accumulation, the areas acquired a particular significance within the domestic arrangements and came to be regarded as locales devoted to the remembrance and veneration of the dead members of the community.

Larsson has argued that late Mesolithic cemeteries in Scandinavia may '...be interpreted as marking a territory where the existence of antecedents' remains motivates the society's claim to traditionally-owned rights' (Larsson 1989a, 213). In coastal regions such rights may well have included access to fishing zones, shellfish banks and flint or stone raw materials; inland hunting territories may well have been similarly guarded. Thus, the emergence of cemeteries against the background of a desire to protect the community's resources need not be excluded as a factor. On the other hand, we are still unclear about the precise nature of the Mesolithic settlements. While many scholars argue that there was a strong degree of sedentism, it is far from clear whether sites such as Vedbæk and Skateholm, or indeed the numerous shell-middens, were occupied seasonally or all year round. If the sites were part of a larger seasonal settlement pattern then the remains of the dead, deliberately interred on these sites, may have helped to lay claim to the local resources. If, on the other hand, people lived there all the year round – even if at times this involved only a small caretaker group – then the territorial and resource arguments are not so strong.

As far as north-western Europe is concerned, the sixth millennium BC was a period of unpredictable natural changes. The evidence from Skateholm, as well as other coastal locations, shows clearly that at intervals people had to move to higher locations to escape the rising sea. While this did not in itself result in any dramatic change of lifestyle, Larsson has suggested that these environmental changes – for example the disappearance of old fishing areas and the appearance of new ones – must have had a profound effect on the conceptual world of the hunter-gatherers; they grappled not only with physical but also with mental stress. The placement of the dead in the midst of the living may thus reflect a claim on resources that was not directed at neighbouring communities but at nature itself.

In general terms, the Scandinavian and Breton cemeteries are coeval with the spread in central Europe of the Danubian farmers. It is not suggested here that the Danubians had a direct influence upon the late Mesolithic burial practices – our review of the evidence has demonstrated ample differences between the two. However, we discussed earlier (chapter 1) the various ways in which hunter-gatherers and incoming farmers may have been in direct or indirect contact with one another, with the impact of that contact unlikely to have been confined to the economic sphere. Indeed, the appearance of farming in large swathes of central Europe may have had a very profound influence on all other aspects of hunter-gatherer life; their social organisation, art and ritual beliefs would have been susceptible to change long before their economy.

In this context the dynamic nature of the Mesolithic burial customs – again seen dramatically at Skateholm – does suggest that funerary practices were subject to modification: influenced by natural events, by changing cosmology as well as by ideas deriving from different cultural worlds. The presence in some Danish Ertebølle graves of Danubian *Schuhleistenkeile* has been noted many times. Is it a coincidence that red deer antlers are no longer used in the younger Skateholm cemetery, that stone-pecked axes are placed with some males and that two-fifths of the dead were buried in the crouched position typical of the Danubian sphere? While the burial customs at Téviec and Höedic are deeply rooted in the earlier Mesolithic traditions (red deer antler, shell jewellery) many of the dead were placed in a crouched position, which equally may echo distant influence from further to the east.

Water was an important element in the Mesolithic beliefs, not merely by virtue of providing a livelihood or being the abode of spirits (the earliest votive deposits in lakes and waterlogged marshy areas date precisely from this period), but as one of three natural elements in the hunter-gatherer cosmology. Its importance in funerary customs is strongly implied in the boat burials (the journey of the dead by boat to the other world is a well-known motif of later Nordic mythology). Larsson has argued that site locations – be they islands, coasts or sea inlets – were at the centre of hunter-gatherer cosmology, which combined water, sky and land. It was there, where these elements met naturally, that sacred places could be established; the fact that people lived their daily lives on these sites as well did not detract from their sanctity.

The Breton shell-middens along the Atlantic coast were placed in equally dramatic locations. While the fluctuation in sea level need not have been perceived within any single generation, the dramatic twice-daily ebb and flow must have been a natural phenomenon with a powerful impact on the world-view of these coastal dwellers. Chris Scarre, writing in the context of Neolithic tombs placed close to the coastline, referred to the tidal regime as an '…evocative physical metaphor for the transition between life and death' (Scarre 2002, 100). It hardly needs saying that it would have been an equally apt metaphor during the time the shell-middens were occupied. Indeed, the metaphor at the end of the Mesolithic may have been double – the ocean encroaching from the west and a new way of life from the east.

Intramural burial is not just a feature of the north-west European Mesolithic. Review of Neolithic burials in general is not directly relevant to our present study, but we have already seen that the arrangements for the burial of some of the Danubian dead reflect a pattern similar to that observed among the hunter-gatherers. While true cemeteries, located some distance away from the actual habitations, were common throughout the whole Danubian area, there is ample evidence of burial within the settlements. Jeunesse has argued that the latter custom was characteristic of the western LBK, particularly of the Paris Basin, but settlement burials are found everywhere (Veit 1992). The later Danubian groups also buried their dead within the settlements: such is the case with the Lengyel communities on the southern fringes of the North European Plain, for example at Brześć Kujawski and at other settlements of this group. Indeed, as I have demonstrated elsewhere (Midgley 1992, 409-10) even within the TRB culture some dead continued to be buried within the settlements.

Veit's discussion of the settlement burials has centred on, among other things, the interpretation of the sort of individuals who were subject to the interment there. Children may well represent a very special group of those buried on the Danubian settlements as their remains are found in intimate association with houses. However, Veit has also suggested that individuals of low social prestige and those who, for some reason or other, found themselves on the edge of society might have been buried in settlements rather than cemeteries. Curiously enough, precisely the same idea has recently been put forward for the interpretation of the Mesolithic cemeteries, with Strassburg arguing that Skateholm, Vedbæk and similar localities were not normal cemeteries but places devoted to dealing with the anomalous dead – women who perished in childbirth, the old, shamans and others who presented a particular danger to the 'normal' community; those who transgressed social norms could seek refuge there (Strassburg 2000, 229-85).

There has been considerably less discussion devoted to the emergence of cemeteries within the Danubian sphere. Indeed, in the late nineteenth- and early twentieth-century researches into the LBK, the settlement interments were regarded as the more archaic form of burial (Veit 1992). Most scholars today comment on the fact that cemeteries appear in the later stages of the *Linearbandkeramik*, but the Vedrovice cemetery (which began during the local LBK Ib phase and could be dated as early as 5500-5300 BC; Podborský *et al.* 2002, 317) suggests that, in some areas at least, cemeteries could appear early within the local sequence.

The idea of a relationship between the community and its critical resources has been evoked in discussions although, against the background of our knowledge of the LBK economy, it is difficult to think of the loess lands as a critical resource, apart perhaps from the labour invested in the initial creation of fields and pastures. Indeed, if the ancestral presence were deemed necessary to the claim on land, one would have expected the cemeteries to be one of the earliest features in the newly settled areas at a time when such claims may have been important; but, clearly, this is not the case everywhere.

Modderman has also evoked the idea of a territory, but in a very different sense. Although he argued that theoretically cemeteries would arise in a society in which the concept of territory begins to play a role, it was people's desire to be buried 'in their "own" ground', assuring their belonging to what 'is home to them' (Modderman 1988, 118).

Ian Hodder (1990), in his interpretations of the Neolithic, developed a powerful metaphor for the opposition between the home (*domus*) and the wild (*agrios*). This opposition was symbolised in south-eastern Europe by a complex of domestic features (houses, hearths, figurines, ovens, burials and women) and the largely culturally unrepresented wild. By the time the Neolithic reached central Europe there developed a different symbolism; the creation of cemeteries outside the village was a process of uncoupling of the ancestors and the house. By placing at least some of the dead out in the *agrios,* a new dimension was added – that of the communal. This process created new conceptual boundaries and, indeed, we may suggest further that it set the stage for subsequent developments, of which monumentality was to be one.

Danubian cemeteries have also provided a source for an enquiry into the social structure of these early farming communities. An early model proposed by Pavúk in 1972 was based on his analysis of the Slovakian cemetery at Nitra. Among the total of 73 tombs, 68 were anthropologically identifiable. Among these only five tombs – all of elderly males – stood out from the rest by virtue of richer grave goods. Consequently, Pavúk argued for a predominantly egalitarian society in which personal power was vested with elderly men, assuming the 'Big Man' role in economic and political community life. Such positions were not hereditary, as was clear from the negligible treatment of the Nitra children. This model was subsequently adopted by many scholars who continue to regard the *Linearbandkeramik* as a society in which age and sex were the only important social determinants, and where there was no evidence of social competition within or between village communities (Lichardus-Itten *et al.* 1985; Lüning 1988; Coudart 1993; Milisauskas 1986).

Modderman (1970, 1988) argued, on the contrary, that the LBK society was not as egalitarian as had been assumed. He ascribed differences in the treatment of some of the dead to their different social status, and also argued that the decreasing number of large houses in each settlement phase was indicative of a small group of families who were socially privileged; this model was developed further by van de Velde's (1979) study of the Elsloo settlement.

Over the past two decades new discoveries from cemeteries as well as settlements have progressively shown that the Nitra model – whatever its merits with reference to that particular cemetery – is not applicable to the whole of the LBK, and recently the French scholar Christian Jeunesse has published a number of papers analysing the social structure of the cemeteries in which he argues for considerable inequality within the early Danubian communities.

According to Jeunesse, the trend among the early Danubian burial practices was for a qualitative and quantitative increase of items deposited with the dead, irrespective of the regional preferences for specific grave goods. For example, where pottery was commonly placed in graves, the number of pots increased over time: at the early Danubian cemetery of Vedrovice the maximum of vessels placed with an individual was five (in grave no.69/78), although normally the dead were provided with only one or two pots, while in the later Danubian contexts up to nine pots (Worms-Rheingewann), and even twelve (Praha-Bubeneč), could be placed in one grave (Jeunesse 1996b, 264).

Differences between individuals became more pronounced, and some of the dead clearly stood out from the rest by virtue of their grave goods; in contrast to the Nitra model, women and children were not excluded from this category. At Vedrovice, which dates early in the LBK, the grave of a child of four to five years of age (grave no.39/76) was classed among one of the richest there; it contained many grave goods including a pot, an armband of Spondylus shells, and eight flint blade fragments. We have already noted the young woman from the same cemetery buried with extraordinary jewellery of Spondylus and marble. Cemeteries in Alsace and in Bavaria also provide rich graves of women and young children. Among the 29 graves at Essenbach (Bavaria) there are two rich graves (one adult male and one child of six to seven years of age), at Ensisheim four out of 24 graves (one male, one female and two children), and at Mulhouse-Est among the six better equipped graves two are of children, three of women and one of an adult male (Jeunesse 1996b, 256-8). A similar situation is known from the Paris Basin, where children are also well endowed with grave goods, for example the two- to five-year-old child at Larzicourt (Marne; *ibid*.). The graves from Mulhouse-Est, which so fascinated Modderman, show that contemporary women could live different lives: the one buried in grave no.14 was of a delicate build and buried with elaborate shell jewellery, while the individual in grave no.15 seems to have spent her life doing hard physical work and was given merely a couple of bone rings (Modderman 1988, 121).

Whether these differences indicate the existence of vertically stratified societies continues to be a matter for discussion. While Jeunesse has argued that in the later LBK power and social standing were hereditary and that these communities approximated to ethnographically known chiefdoms, others have stressed that marked differences between individuals and groups may be equally apparent in communities which are neither egalitarian nor stratified – the so-called transegalitarian societies (Bogucki 2003). Among such groups individual power, prestige and status are easily achieved; they are short-lived and not passed from one generation to the next as there are no mechanisms for such transfers, but loose alliances, and sometimes fierce competition, play important economic and social roles.

Evidence for competitiveness has been particularly noted towards the end of the LBK with, among other things, exotic objects such as stone mace heads and perforated double-edged axes (predecessors of the later battle axes?) making their appearance in some graves; these are interpreted as items of male prestige closely connected with war. While such prestige may have been very important in the social context, it seems to have been a result of very real and dramatic events. The evidence of mass burials discovered at Aspern, Talheim and Herxheim points to a very traumatic period around 5100-5000 BC. The Talheim burial of 34 individuals represents an entire community – men, women and children, many of whom suffered powerful blows to their heads – but it is not clear who they were: did they live in a nearby LBK settlement or were they, perhaps, a small group of final hunter-gatherers in the vicinity? What does seem certain is that their lives ended in violence on a scale not witnessed before. The finds from Aspern, in Austria – where up to 300 individuals, with young women conspicuously missing, were buried in a disorganised manner in an enclosure ditch – as well as the find from Herxheim – where broken-up remains of up to 450 individuals were buried in two ditches – confirm that the end of the *Linearbandkeramik* was a time of strife and violence (Farruggia 2002).

The causes of these difficulties are not easily identified in the archaeological record, but there are some pointers. We have grown accustomed to considering enclosures as largely ceremonial in nature and, indeed, this seems to be the case with many central European sites. Nevertheless, some scholars argue that the enclosing of the late LBK villages was for purposes of defence. Keeley and Cahen (1989), for example, made a strong plea for the defensive function of the Belgian enclosures at Darion, Longchamps and Oleye, with the high proportion of burnt houses at the latter site possibly indicating raids on the village. Farruggia (2002) has pointed to the construction of wells and water reservoirs, the abandonment of some villages and the desecration of graves. The appearance of axe hoards at the end of the LBK, the presence of combat weapons in the graves and the desire for the expression of victory may be taken as evidence for dramatic and uncertain times around 5100-5000 BC.

The causes of the crisis may have been economic, social, political or possibly even environmental in nature, or indeed a combination of all these factors. These dramatic upheavals – so poignantly illustrated by the mass graves – resulted in the emergence of new regional Danubian groups. The archaeological evidence reveals even greater status differences in these contexts, the appearance of new forms of public monuments (Rondel enclosures consisting of circular arrangements of banks, ditches and palisades), different settlement forms and new material culture; all these features point to profound changes midway through the Danubian cycle. These changes, however, carried within themselves the seeds of further cultural adjustments and transformations, among which the subsequent monumental funerary practices created some of the most powerful images of Neolithic Europe.

CHAPTER 4

LONG BARROW CEMETERIES: MOUNDS AND THEIR CONSTRUCTION

The issues concerning the origins of the TRB and Cerny cultures, which we have discussed in chapter 2, naturally do not revolve merely around the identification of novel material culture and new economy. Significantly they also involve the social and symbolic processes that were taking place in the middle of the fifth millennium BC. One manifestation of these processes is the emergence of new funerary rituals most poignantly expressed in the construction of large funerary earthworks – the long mounds.

While long mounds★ – that is earthen mounds with timber burial chambers – have been known in north-western Europe for a long time, their significance in the development of the Neolithic monumental funerary tradition has always been overshadowed by the scholarly attention directed mainly towards megaliths (Greek *megas*: large, *lithos*: stone). Megaliths, with their spectacular stone-built chambers, indeed represent the most tangible remains of the Neolithic populations. On the other hand, the use of timber and earth as the principal medium for the construction of long barrows – the former prone to quick natural decay, and the latter easily subject to destruction through several millennia of ploughing and other industrial activities – has led to these monuments remaining largely in the background of archaeological research.

★In English language literature terms such as 'earthen long barrow' and 'unchambered long barrow' have been used for a long time to describe burial mounds which do not reveal stone-built chambers. While the latter term is no longer correct, terms such as long mound, long barrow and earthen long barrow will be used interchangeably to denote monuments which do not have stone-built chambers. When a stone-built chamber is present, this will be clear from the context. Continental counterparts include: *Hünenbett ohne Kammer, kammerlose Hünenbett, grobowiec bezkomorowy* and *langehoj med jordgrav*; the French usually use the term *tertre tumulaire* for the Armorican monuments and *le type Passy* for monuments in and around the Paris Basin.

I have argued on many occasions that one of the problems of interpreting the origins and function of the monumental funerary tradition, which emerges in north-west Europe at around the middle of the fifth millennium BC, stems precisely from this deeply embedded belief that stone-built monuments – the 'true megaliths' – are fundamentally different from other contemporary burial structures. In my view, one of the most important results of recent decades of research is the accumulation of evidence for the existence of well-established early timber mortuary architecture – inconspicuous under its name of the earthen long barrows – which has extended the concept of monumental funerary architecture beyond the bounds of stone-built megalithic tombs. It is therefore fundamental that we should think in terms of the north-west European monumental funerary tradition: with some structures indeed built in stone, others in timber and others still employing both timber and stone in their construction. It is the monumentality of the funerary structures, and not the raw materials used in their construction, that must be considered as significant (Midgley 1985, 1997a, 1997b, 2000, forthcoming).

The spectacular discoveries during the 1980s in the south Paris Basin, and in other regions of France, of monumental cemeteries which do not contain any major 'megalithic' elements, as well as continuing discoveries of such monuments in areas where their presence has been well attested in the past, are once again focusing scholarly attention on this important phenomenon.

BRIEF HISTORY OF RESEARCH

The results of the nineteenth- and early twentieth-century research on long barrows were discussed in my earlier work (Midgley 1985) dealing with northern Europe. In summary, however, it may be pertinent to remind ourselves of one or two aspects of these early investigations once again.

The nineteenth century was the 'heyday' of local archaeological societies in Schleswig-Holstein, Mecklenburg and Pomerania, and their records are often the only source of information on long-destroyed monuments. Thus, surveys carried out in 1825 by von Plön on behalf of the local archaeological society (*Gesellschaft für pommersche Geschichte und Altertumskunde*) in Western Pomerania, north-west Poland, revealed the existence of massive necropoli of dozens of barrows (*colour plate 9*). Over 150 mounds were, for example, recorded in the vicinity of the modern town of Pyrzyce, of which only a few scattered examples survive today; all mounds were apparently delimited by kerbs built of glacial boulders, but it is no longer possible to ascertain which might have contained timber-built chambers. We may also recall the work of Robert Beltz who, at the turn of the twentieth century, catalogued about 120 barrows in Mecklenburg and divided them into those with stone chambers and those without (*Hünenbetten ohne Steinkammern*; Beltz 1910). His concern that insufficient evidence prevented him from determining whether or not the lack of stone chamber was an original feature, was quite exceptional for that period and it took many years before this issue was raised again.

There are no precise records for the destruction of the earthen long mounds in north Germany, but both Ebbesen (1986) and Hoika (1990) comment on the massive destruction of megaliths, a process which would equally have obliterated burial mounds with timber chambers. The last two decades of research in Denmark, where the long mounds do not form cemeteries but are found either singly or in pairs, have demonstrated the destructive power of past agricultural activities but, interestingly, have also shown that appropriate field research methods and re-evaluation of older records can help to account for many previously misinterpreted monuments.

Long mounds with small, slab-built cists (*tertres tumulaires*) have been recognised in Brittany since the early nineteenth century, some even noted and described by that most flamboyant of ancient monuments inspectors, Prosper Mérimée, in the 1830s. The astonishing diversity and richness of megalithic remains in this one region has, even more than elsewhere, overshadowed the rather less impressive *tertres*, with their tiny, slab-built cists and chambers, although Le Rouzic's investigations at the beginning of the twentieth century did at least establish them as a type (Boujot and Cassen 1992). Detailed concern with the Breton *tertres* is really beyond the scope of this book,★ although some comparisons with the area will be inevitable. Within the context of the historical background we may, however, profit by quoting Stuart Piggott's comments in his early discussion of the stone cists typical of long mounds in the region of Carnac: 'Making a box of small stones to contain the remains of the dead is an idea as obvious in a stony country as is digging a hole in regions of softer subsoil' (Piggott 1937, 447); alas, such an obvious idea has not always been recognised in practice.

The scale of recent discoveries in central France has been quite staggering. Aerial photographs taken in the 1950s by Parruzot in the Yonne river valley, particularly the photographs of Passy, revealed curious elongated features which he called '*épingles à cheveux*' although he did regard them as natural rather than cultural phenomena, related to the underground movement of water in the alluvial sands (Delor *et al.* 1997, 382). After the first season of rescue excavations at Passy in 1978, it became clear that these elongated features represented ditches enclosing areas with burials, although the tentative presentation of these as Neolithic, during the Caen Neolithic colloquium of 1983, was greeted with general scepticism. The cemetery at Passy was excavated largely between 1982 and 1986 (Duhamel 1997; Duhamel and Mordant 1997; Duhamel and Prestreau 1991), and Balloy – discovered from the air in 1985 – was excavated

★Readers interested in the most recent investigations of some of the Breton *tertres* may consult Cassen *et al.* 2000 which, while nominally a report on the excavation of the Lannec er Gadouer barrow, offers a wide-ranging discussion of many relevant issues.

between 1987 and 1991 (Augereau *et al.* 1992; Augereau and Mordant 1993; Mordant 1997).

Since then re-evaluation of old aerial photographs as well as new aerial surveys, followed by the excavation of endangered sites, have completely altered the picture of the Cerny burial and ceremonial practices. In addition to the sites from the Yonne and Seine area, monumental cemeteries are now known from the Plaine de Caen; nine sites are reported from here although only two, Fleury-sur-Orne and Rots, have been subject to excavation (Chancerel *et al.* 1992; Desloges 1997). They have even been found in the truly 'megalithic' zone of the west of France, as the recent excavations of La Jardelle cemetery, Vienne, have demonstrated (Pautreau *et al.* 2003). Most French scholars today accept that these cemeteries belong to the Neolithic Cerny culture, although their monumental nature is not accepted by all (Mohen 2003).

New sites continue to appear elsewhere. We may note proper recent recognition of this phenomenon in central Moravia, where at least 17 cemeteries are known today. Some of the Moravian sites have been known since the early twentieth century (Slatinky) while others were discovered recently: Otaslavice and Drahanovice, each with at least twenty mounds, and Náměšt' na Hané with 58 mounds (Šmíd 2000, 2003). Long barrows also continue to be discovered in Poland, most recently in the south at Zagaj Stradowski and Malice Košcielne (Burchard 1998; Bargieł *et al.* 1998, 1999; Florek and Libera 1997).

Moreover, one would expect that, in the future, the intensive aerial survey in the area of the former East Germany will discover similar, long-vanished sites. Saxony, for example, can now claim an amazing concentration of the circular Rondel-type enclosures of which none were known prior to the aerial survey launched in the early 1990s (Stäuble 2002). The areas most in need are, of course, the regions of the north German lowland – especially Mecklenburg and Brandenburg – where the TRB culture was as precocious as in Kujavia. It is inconceivable that the long barrow cemeteries in Kujavia and Western Pomerania should be an isolated phenomenon and new discoveries, while possibly endangering current interpretations, are indeed most eagerly awaited.

The distribution of long barrows in continental Europe is vast (*19*): from southern Scandinavia in the north to Moravia in the south, and stretching westwards to Normandy and deep into central France, with long mounds now equally prominent along the Atlantic façade; the Channel Islands form a convenient link between the continental and British barrows. Within this distribution, however, the monumental cemeteries – conglomerations of a dozen or more barrows – make a highly significant appearance on the periphery of the disintegrating Danubian world: in the regions of Kujavia and Western Pomerania in Poland, in France on the Plaine de Caen, along the river valleys of the Yonne and Seine, and possibly also in Moravia. These are precisely the areas of intensive cultural contacts between the indigenous hunter–gatherers

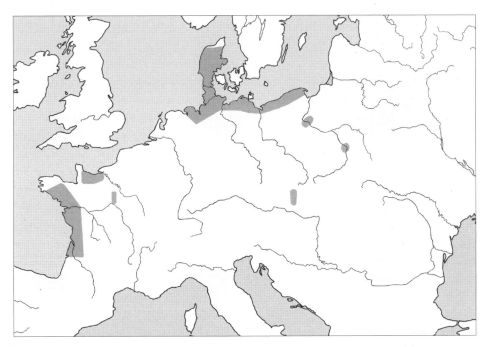

19 Distribution of long barrow monumental cemeteries in north-west Europe. *Midgley 1985; Constantin* et al. *1997*

and the Danubian farmers, and here the barrow cemeteries constitute a prelude to the monumentality of the Neolithic funerary tradition.

While these barrow cemeteries display considerable variety, with elements of design, construction and rituals clearly reflecting both natural and cultural conditions prevalent in different regions, certain features transcend geographical boundaries emphasising the wider, European character of this phenomenon.

LOCATION OF THE LONG BARROWS: NATURAL AND CULTURAL LANDSCAPES

In my initial research on the north European long barrows (Midgley 1985), I discussed the various aspects of location and the reader is referred to that work for details. However, against the background of new research, especially the discoveries in France, as well as new theoretical considerations, the location in the natural landscape and the spatial relationship between the mounds and settlements are two aspects which may profitably be reviewed in a fresh light.

While it would be incorrect to suggest that barrow location across north-west Europe reflects only one or two specific patterns – we can point to clustered, dispersed or individual distributions everywhere – certain regularities, which appear to be supra-regional, indicate that the placing of barrows was far from haphazard. The location of long mound cemeteries in particular suggests that 'islands' – natural elevations within a relatively boggy, marshy and waterlogged environment – may have been deliberately selected for burial purposes. Such landscapes were important to hunting and gathering communities and their continued significance – economic as well as spiritual – for the TRB and Cerny farming communities should not be underestimated.

The Kujavian cemeteries are located within a heavily glaciated landscape of gently undulating hills surrounded by a network of lakes and slow-flowing rivers. The cemetery of Sarnowo is located on a slight sandy elevation (of about 5m) above the confluence of the Zgłowiączka river and a small, peaty stream. Detailed geomorphological surveys are lacking for other Kujavian cemeteries, but in general they were placed in similar environments. Gaj was located on a slight elevation above a peaty meadow; wet meadows stretched to the south of Leśniczówka, and postglacial meltwater valleys surrounded the sites of Zberzyn and Zberzynek. Such a consistent association of Kujavian cemeteries with low-lying, boggy and marshy environments suggests that landscapes closely associated with water were an important factor in their siting.

This relationship, between the monumental cemeteries and water, is even more emphatically demonstrated when we consider the French sites. The rivers Seine and Yonne, in whose valleys the majority of the Cerny cemeteries have been discovered so far, are well known for their meandering courses, as much today as in prehistory. In the vicinity of Balloy, small, sandy-gravel hills form islands separated by ancient channels of the Seine, now filled with alluvium and peat. Aerial photographs of numerous cemeteries discovered along the river Yonne, from its confluence with the Seine in the north to just south of Escolives-Sainte-Camille – a stretch of about 120km as the crow flies – suggest that the location of cemeteries was very closely related to the meanderings of this river (*20*; Delor *et al.* 1997).

At Passy, the Yonne valley expands through a huge meander to create an elevation which is about 7km long and at least 1km wide. The cemetery was located upon a slight sandy-gravel elevation bordered by the Yonne in the west and the today silted-up palaeochannel in the east (*21*). At Escolives-Sainte-Camille (*colour plate 10*) the alluvial plain of the Yonne has cut through the Jurassic limestone plateau. The palaeochannels to the east and west of the cemetery, seen in aerial photographs and confirmed through excavation, ceased to be active by the late Bronze Age. There is little doubt that such elevations were seasonally cut off by the flooding river from the surrounding landscape, becoming, at least temporarily, real islands.

20 Opposite above: Distribution of long barrow cemeteries in the Seine and Yonne valleys. *Duhamel & Mordant 1997*

21 Opposite below: Location of the long barrow cemetery at Passy within the Yonne meander. *Duhamel & Prestreau 1987*

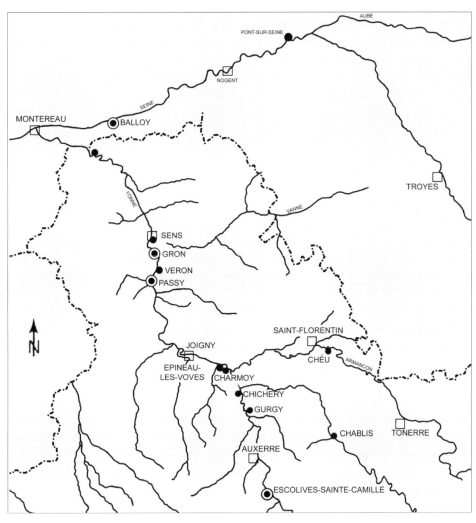

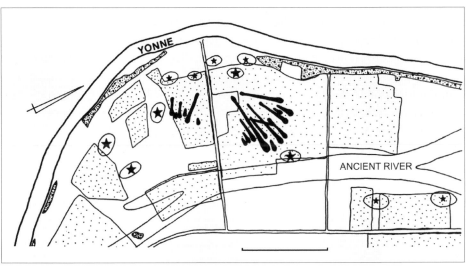

We may also remind ourselves that, at the other end of the barrow distribution, in Denmark, locations were chosen with similar conditions in mind. A classic example is offered by the site of Barkær, on the Djursland Peninsula in Jutland, where a pair of barrows, each nearly 90m long, was located on a hill in the sea inlet of Kolind Sund; many other Danish barrows are close to large expanses of water.

One other aspect of the location of long barrows, sometimes interspersed with megaliths, should be noted: that of long-distance linear arrangements. The nineteenth-century descriptions of Pomeranian barrows recorded by von Plön suggest that, in the vicinity of Pyrzyce, they formed chains of cemeteries at the edge of the morainic plateau, occasionally reaching deep towards local watersheds. Such arrangements, with reference to megaliths, have been commented upon by many scholars, most notably Bakker who, as mentioned previously, studied their distribution in relation to ancient routes (Bakker 1976). Indeed, the location of monumental cemeteries along the river Yonne, while not strictly speaking 'linear', may perhaps be seen as a reflection of the importance of this river in providing a major communication route: not only to the north but, via the Rhône, to the Mediterranean lands in the south.

As a less dramatic but equally important (at least in terms of its longevity) example of a linear distribution, in which long mounds with timber-built chambers were among early components, we may just mention the 4km-long string of 75 mounds built on the ground moraine in the vicinity of Flintbek, near Kiel (Zich 1993). The linear arrangement (today largely destroyed) which crossed the promontory around Lindebjerg on north-west Zealand (Liversage 1981) is a good example of the importance of marking even relatively short, convenient and safe routes of passage.

The location of the cemeteries upon abandoned settlements and ploughed fields is another feature of pan-European occurrence. The cemetery at Sarnowo (*22*) was raised upon an abandoned TRB settlement, possibly when the inhabitants chose to move onto slightly higher and drier land directly to the north. Foundations of small, rectangular houses, together with traces of an ancient ploughed field, have been found underneath the earthen mounds. Although scholarly opinion with respect to the ploughed field at this site is strongly divided (Midgley 1985; Sherratt 1987; Niesiołowska-Śreniowska 1999) there are other examples of such location. One of the two recently excavated barrows at Zagaj Stradowski, in southern Poland, has clearly been placed upon an old field (Burchard 1998, Fig. 2). Moreover, many of the individual Danish long mounds were unarguably placed upon previously cultivated fields, with plough-marks surviving under the protection of the mound (Thrane 1982), and this tradition continued well into the TRB with many megalithic chambers built in similar locations.*

*Readers may follow a polemical discussion between Peter Rowley-Conwy and Kristian Kristiansen on the significance of plough-marks under burial mounds in *Antiquity* 61, 263-6 and *Antiquity* 64, 322-7.

22 Plan of the cemetery at
Sarnowo in Kujavia

In Kujavia, apart from the above clear instance at Sarnowo, the barrow at Gaj was placed on an earlier settlement, and possibly Leśniczówka and Zberzynek cemeteries and, in Western Pomerania, several of the Łupawa barrows as well as Wartin, were built on old settlement sites. In northern Germany, the cemetery of long mounds at Sachsenwald, not far from the modern city of Hamburg, and the long barrow at Tosterglope, Lüneburg, were similarly placed upon abandoned settlements. Equally impressive numbers of examples are available from Scandinavia: the two barrows at Barkær and barrows at Lindebjerg, Mosegården, Konens Høj and Stengade are the most obvious coastal as well as inland sites, where the barrow building followed upon the settlement.

Recent investigations around the shell-midden at Bjørnsholm, on the Limfjord, have shown not only that there was a TRB settlement upon and next to the old Ertebølle midden but that a grave, subsequently covered with a long mound, was constructed just to the rear of the midden. Moreover, the grave was not just within the settlement area but, significantly, it was dug into an old TRB house foundation (Andersen S.H. and Johansen 1990, 54 and Fig. 4), making it absolutely clear that such a placement was intentional.

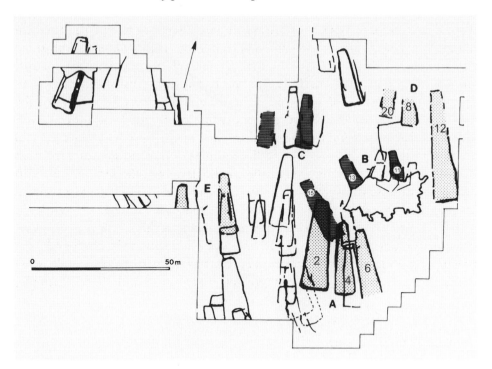

23 Plan of the settlement at Brześć Kujawski

In the south Paris Basin the situation is similar, although the cultural context is slightly different. So far there is no indication that the cemetery at Escolives-Sainte-Camille was located in the immediate vicinity of any ancient habitation, although some evidence for Danubian settlement, burials and a largely destroyed enclosure has been recorded about 2km to the north of the cemetery. The sandy-gravel 'island' upon which the cemetery at Passy was constructed supported both an earlier Villeneuve-Saint-Germain and a Cerny settlement. The precise chronological relationship between the Cerny settlement and the cemetery is not clear, but in both cases the settlement traces appear largely outwith the two groups of barrows (*21*).

At this stage, it is perhaps also useful to note the spatial layout of some of the monumental cemeteries. The arrangement of barrows within the cemeteries – seen as far apart as Kujavia and the Yonne valley – is reminiscent of the spatial arrangements of houses in villages of the late Danubian settlements in these regions. In Kujavia this pattern can be demonstrated by comparing the layout of barrows at Sarnowo with the arrangement of houses at Brześć Kujawski (*22* and *23*). The two sites are about 15km apart and may well have been contemporary towards the final stages of occupation of the Brześć Kujawski village. Similar arrangements are characteristic of a number of other Kujavian cemeteries, for example at Obałki, Leśniczówka and Wietrzychowice (Midgley 1985, Figs. 23 and 24).

In the south Paris Basin the barrows are reminiscent of individual Danubian houses by virtue of their shape and delineation by ditch segments, with some medium-sized barrows at Escolives, for example, offering a perfect dimensional and conceptual match (*24*). Although the layout of the Passy cemetery gives the overall impression of a fan-like arrangement (*25*), detailed analysis of the layout of the barrows has identified a more complex underlying pattern, with individual barrows seemingly grouped in twos or threes (Chambon 2003). In the northern sector of the cemetery (Sablonnière), clear sub-groups, each with its own orientation, can be seen in the parallel layout of the monuments: thus one distinct group is formed by barrows 1, 2 and 3, another by 4 and 5 (barrow 5 being the longest in the cemetery at over 300m), and another by barrows 7, 8 and 9. An anomaly, in terms of size for this sector, is the group of small, pear-shaped monuments 10 and 11. In the southern sector (Richebourg), the groupings are much more discrete on account of the orientation as well as the alteration of the monuments. Nevertheless, barrows 18 and 19, for example,

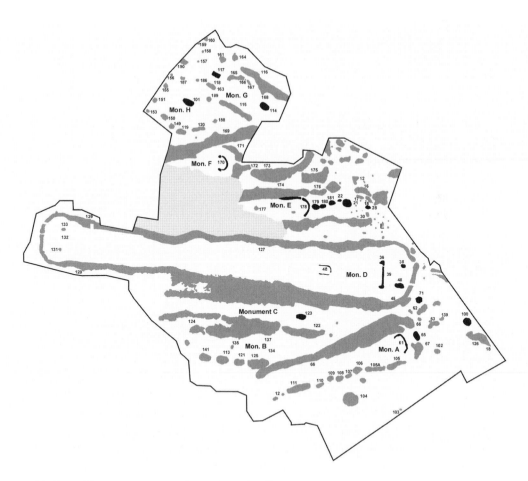

24 Plan of the cemetery at Escolives-Sainte-Camille

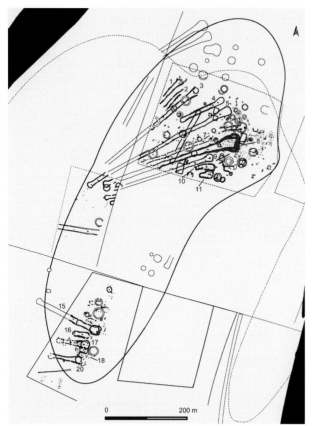

25 Plan of the cemetery at Passy.
Duhamel 1997

seem to form one unit and, through their final extensions, barrows 17 and 20 may ultimately have been intended as another such grouping. If the barrows at Passy were indeed modelled upon the Danubian long houses, the exaggerated, well-nigh gigantic, size of the monuments suggests that additional symbolism may have been involved.

It is, however, the site of Balloy that offers the most spectacular evidence. Here a late Danubian settlement of several trapezoidal houses was inhabited at about 4700 BC. After the village was abandoned for a while, a community of the Cerny culture used the same location to create, around 4500-4450 BC, a large ceremonial centre devoted to burial and other rituals: they constructed a causewayed enclosure (which overlaid two Villeneuve-Saint-Germain houses) and, to the north-west, they built a monumental cemetery of 17 barrows (*26*). At least five of these were placed directly on top of the earlier houses; their orientation is exactly the same, the barrows cover the houses precisely and these house remains were much better preserved that those that remained uncovered. The evidence from Balloy demonstrates beyond any doubt that, while ruined, the late Danubian houses were still visible on the surface to guide the positioning of the burial mounds some 200 years after the settlement had been abandoned.

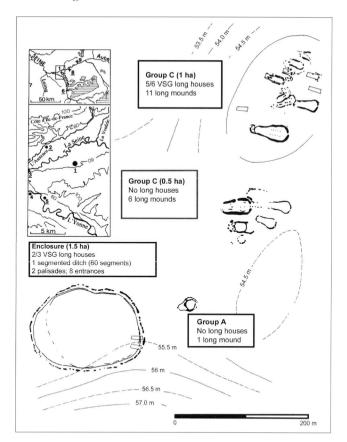

26 Plan of the ceremonial complex at Balloy. *Mordant 1997*

CONSTRUCTION OF THE LONG BARROWS

It is evident that within the continental long-mound tradition there was a pool of architectural and constructional ideas since, even on a single cemetery, there may be a considerable variety of forms, with some features clearly related to the local conditions prevailing in each region. The shape of the mounds varies in outline from oval, rectangular, trapezoidal to triangular, with lengths ranging from as little as 20m to over 300m; the width is rarely greater than 10m. In principle there are three main ways of delimiting the mound: within a stone setting, by means of ditch segments and by timber palisades, although each architectural style has numerous variations, often employed at the same site.

In central France, a region not well endowed with stone for building material, the barrows were defined by pits and ditches, some of which may have had timber posts placed in them forming a sort of palisade. One of the principal problems in the interpretation of the sequence of construction of the French monumental cemeteries is the nearly complete lack of stratigraphy and overlap between very closely spaced mounds. However, the cemetery at Passy, where altogether 23 long mounds were fully or partly excavated, does provide slight evidence for relative stratigraphy between some of the monuments. Pascal

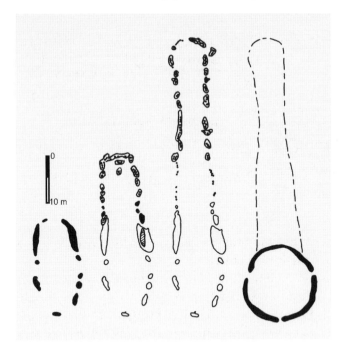

27 Left Duhamel's model of the evolution of barrow building at Passy. *Duhamel 1997*

28 Opposite Plan of the Flintbek long barrow. *Zich 1993*

Duhamel, the excavator of the southern section of the cemetery (Richebourg), was able to observe slight overlaps between barrows 15, 17 and 20 – information which enabled him to put forward a hypothesis for the sequence and evolution of the long mounds (*27*; Duhamel 1997). While such a developmental sequence cannot definitely be established at other French monumental cemeteries, numerous elements of Duhamel's model are in fact evident at other sites.

Duhamel proposed an architectural development sequence which started with relatively short, oval or trapezoidal mounds of between 20m and 30m in length, delimited by series of pits. There then followed the creation of longer structures (at least 50m in length) limited by pits, by ditch segments or, in some cases, by both. This, in turn, led to progressive elongation of monuments (the longest Passy barrow is over 300m in length). The final stage in the sequence was the construction of circular enclosures, clearly superimposed upon the eastern end of the long mound.

Apart from Passy, the superimposition of circular structures upon the long mounds is well documented at La Jardelle (*colour plate 11*), where this sequence is further supported by the dating of the monuments: the long mounds are dated to the middle of the fifth millennium BC while the circular structures date to the early fourth millennium BC.* At Rots, one of the long mounds has a cairn superimposed upon its south-eastern end (Desloges 1997, Fig. 9) and,

*The long mound A is dated to between 4496 and 4367 BC, long mound B is dated to between 4523 and 4339 BC, the circular structure C dates to between 3959 and 3757 BC and structure D is bracketed by dates between 3349 and 3634 BC (Pautreau *et al.* 2003).

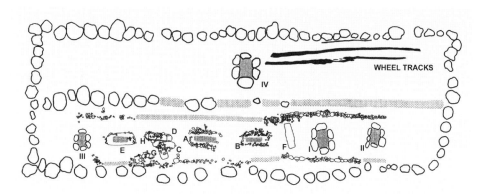

while this structure is different in form from the circular enclosures at Passy and La Jardelle, the principle is exactly the same.

Extensions and alterations of existing mounds are a widespread feature. At least five of the Balloy monuments were extended, most probably to accommodate new burials; the northern ditch of monument A at Escolives-Sainte-Camille was certainly extended in length on at least one occasion, and similar enlargement may apply to monument E (*24*). Such practices can also be documented elsewhere. The meticulous approach of Lidia Gabałówna to the excavation of barrow 8 at Sarnowo has shown that the barrow was extended by 9m to the east, in order to cover two additional graves (Gabałówna 1970; Midgley 1985, 237-8). Of the two barrows at Barkær, the northern barrow was extended on at least one occasion while the southern one was elongated twice, eventually reaching close to 90m in length. The Lindebjerg barrow seems to have been increased in height upon the construction of a second burial chamber, while Bygholm Nørremark offers an excellent example of an aggrandisement, with the original timber enclosure being replicated permanently in stone.

Indeed, we should remind ourselves that alterations – extension, rebuilding, construction of secondary chambers, changes in shape and form – are characteristic not just of earthen long barrows but also of mounds with stone-built megalithic chambers; the nature of stone as a building material preserving such changes in the most dramatic form. The 'megalithic' cemetery at Bougon, the 11 passage-grave mound at Barnanez, the megalithic complex of Le Petit Mont at Arzon and the long mound at Prissé-la-Charrière (the latter still under excavation) are just some of the spectacular examples from north-western France. From northern Europe we may note the long mound at Flintbek; not only did it contain several timber- and stone-built graves but eventually it served as a basis from which a second mound was built in parallel, incidentally covering an ancient track (*28*; Zich 1993). Some of the very long megalithic chambers from the region of Emsland (in excess of 20m in length) may well have resulted from the rebuilding of several shorter graves, and Danish long dolmen mounds may equally have been extended as new chambers were being added.

On the basis of observations from Passy, the delineation of the burial area thus includes several elements: pits, series of pits and ditch segments. At Balloy the ditches enclosing the monuments are of a segmented nature, often inter-rupted and of variable depth; at one of the Fleury barrows the ditch is, in reality, a succession of segments separated by causeways. The ditch of monument A at La Jardelle was equally a series of ditch fragments, just over 2m in length and of differing depth; the smaller of the Gron mounds was also defined by a series of short ditch segments.

Similar constructions can be noted at Escolives-Sainte-Camille. Here the enclosing elements reveal the entire range of possibilities: barrow A was limited by a series of individual pits on the south side and a continuous ditch on the north side, and barrow B followed a similar pattern (*25*). Monument D (*Le Grand Monument*), which is just under 100m in length, appears to have been defined by a single continuous ditch with one narrow gap at the north-east end; a series of transverse and longitudinal sections through the entire southern length of this ditch has demonstrated an equally segmented nature, with indi-vidual stretches differing in length as well as in depth. While it is difficult to assess the sites, which are known exclusively from aerial photographs, the evidence from the excavations, coupled with observation of the plans as seen from the air, suggests that the principle of elongated pits and segmented ditches was used in the definition of long mounds.

Such a manner of space definition is, of course, not unique to the long mounds. It is to be found in the construction of the contemporary causewayed enclosures: the Balloy enclosure adjacent to the cemetery was defined by a series of about 60 pits up to 3m in length. Similar arrangements are known from Villeneuve-la-Guyard, Barbuise-Courtavant and Châtenay-sur-Seine (*12*; Mordant and Simonin 1997). Danish TRB enclosures, of which many examples are known (Sarup and Toftum, to name the most obvious sites), as well as those from northern Germany (Büdelsdorf), were created using exactly the same digging techniques (Andersen N.H. 1997). Indeed, the interrupted ditch construction has a much greater ancestry, going back to the Danubian period. This is just as clearly illustrated by the enclosures from the Paris Basin (Menneville) and from Belgium (Darion, Longchamps) as it is in the consistent presence of lateral pits delimiting the Danubian style houses; the latter emphatically pointing to the morphological similarities between houses of the living and houses of the dead.

The use of timbers – as freestanding posts or in the form of a palisade – is a matter for some discussion. Certain ditch segments at Passy and at Escolives-Sainte-Camille revealed unambiguous traces of posts within either ditch segments or individual pits. Since the posts are not contiguous to one another, either they were freestanding or, more likely, they formed a framework for the horizontal attachment of planks, with such timber walls perhaps serving as a screen for activities in the interior and, after the mound was erected, as its revetment. Both functions at different stages of burial ritual need not be excluded.

The use of timber, at least partly enclosing the interior of the monuments, has been well documented in Denmark, for example at Mosegården, Bygholm Nørremark and Troelstrup, to name but the most obvious examples (Midgley 1985, Figs. 40 and 41). In addition, many of the Danish barrows had a massive timber façade erected at the eastern end of the mound (*ibid.* 123-27). We should also remind ourselves of the two largely forgotten structures from Březno in the Czech Republic (Pleinerová 1971) which offer close parallels to some of the very long French mounds. These two burial enclosures, one about 24m and the other 143.5m long, while not showing any traces of a mound, were delimited by parallel trenches which contained numerous traces of timber posts. The interpretation was rather ambiguous, but the excavator did think in terms of a timber superstructure of some sort rising from the foundation trenches.

In 1985 I argued that some of the Polish structures, such as that at Niedźwiedź where a trapezoidal trench contained numerous timber posts, should be interpreted as long mounds rather than houses. This interpretation has been confirmed by the recent discovery of the two barrows at Zagaj Stradowski: the smaller mound was surrounded by a bedding trench in which traces of about 20 posts were still surviving, while the longer mound had a trench with 180 posts still clearly visible (Burchard 1998, Fig. 2).

Indeed, like the interrupted ditch technique discussed above, timber architecture in north-west Europe was not limited to long mounds. The excavations of the contemporary causewayed enclosures, documented in France, north Germany and southern Scandinavia – in which massive timber palisades had been built and either subsequently dismantled or allowed to rot – demonstrate not just widespread carpentry skills but, more significantly, the importance of timber as a raw material in the overall sphere of ceremonial activities, and this includes even the areas of western France where stone is used to build burial chambers.

In northern Europe, where glaciated erratic boulders were present in abundance, they were largely used instead of timber. The Kujavian and Western Pomeranian long barrows are well known for their stone kerbs over a metre in height (*colour plate 12*), delimiting areas sometimes well in excess of 100m in length. Similar settings of stones were enclosing the long barrows in Mecklenburg. While the boulders were not specifically shaped, efforts were made to place them with the flatter sides to the outside, and there are indications that spaces between them were filled in with smaller stones to create an even outside face.

In these areas the presence of the covering mantle of earth, or a mixture of earth and stones, retained within the surrounding stone kerb is simply not in doubt. While naturally subject to destruction, through the processes of removal

29 Tentative reconstruction of the Passy long barrow cemetery. *Tosello's illustration from the cover of* Résumés des communications *at Colloque International de Nemours*

of the kerb stones and flattening through agricultural activities, the long mounds here are nevertheless sufficiently well preserved to indicate that the area defined by the stone kerb was, at some stage, covered by a massive mound. Although Jażdżewski, speaking in 1969 at the third Atlantic colloquium at Moesgård (Jażdżewski 1973), did state that the material for the mound was extracted from quarry-like ditches flanking the barrows, there is no evidence that the Kujavian long barrows or those in Western Pomerania had quarry ditches. Indeed, the excavations at Zberzyn demonstrated that the earth was scraped from the surface, and this is further supported by the presence of older or contemporary cultural material within many mounds.

The presence or absence of mounds on the French cemeteries is the subject of considerable debate (*29*). As we have already noted, the evidence for the Passy-type French cemeteries is a result of aerial prospection, and none has been detected through any vestiges visible on the surface. This, in itself, indicates a serious destruction process, resulting from a range of past and modern agricultural and industrial activities, although natural erosion factors should not be excluded altogether. Once again, evidence of ditch fills at Passy and Escolives-Sainte-Camille reveals layers that could only have derived from the slippage of the internal mound, although the quantity of the fill itself does not indicate a massive cover. Similar fill, equally scanty in volume, has been noted at one or two monuments at Balloy.

It is not necessary to assume that the French long barrows were covered by massive mounds. Many of the Danish long mounds seem to have been relatively low and, indeed, uneven in height. The greatest volume may have been piled upon the graves and in other parts the mounds may well have been rather lower. However, evidence from Passy reveals that the original ground level, defined by the setting of timber posts, may have been raised by deposition of additional materials. The interior of barrows 10 and 11, excavated by Henri Carré, had been raised, along the entire length of both monuments, by a sand layer between 20 and 25cm in thickness – material clearly different from the original sandy gravel land surface. Several large extraction pits have been noted in the vicinity of these two mounds, although no archaeological materials have been found in any of them.

While examples of such deliberately introduced materials are not present everywhere, there is sufficient evidence across the whole area of the barrow distribution that soils from different environments were intentionally included in the construction of the mounds. We noted earlier the importance of water environments for the location of the monumental cemeteries, and this significance is emphasised even further in the use of water-derived deposits in the construction of mounds. We note this in barrow 9 at Sarnowo, where muddy soil of riverine origin was spread out in a 40cm thick layer at the eastern end, and in the black peaty soil that was deliberately brought in to cover two eastern graves in barrow 8. The two graves at Rogalki were covered with a layer of grey soil containing *Anodon* shells (Midgley 1985, 233). From Denmark we may point to the example of the Storgård IV barrow from north Jutland, where a layer of turf was brought into the palisaded enclosure (Kristensen 1991).

In Brittany, substantial quantities of water-derived silt were used in the construction of the inner core of the Lannec er Gadouer barrow (Cassen *et al.* 2000, figure on page 754). Cassen notes that deposits of this kind already fascinated the nineteenth-century investigators of the Armorican *tertres* (although the wetland origin was not recognised) and points out the deliberate and consistent employment of soils extracted from marshy and boggy environments in the construction of numerous Breton mounds, for example at Er Grah, Le Manio 2, Mané Gardreine, Mané Granvillarec and many others (*ibid.* 153-58).

ARRANGEMENTS AROUND AND WITHIN THE LONG BARROWS

That arrivals at and departures from monuments were important aspects of the funerary ritual is evident from a whole range of features. In my discussion of the Kujavian barrows (Midgley 1985, 81-2) I commented upon the fact that the ground plan of the monuments was not symmetrical but that frequently one of the long sides had been laid out with a characteristic 'kink' at a distance of roughly one-third from the broader, eastern end. This feature is so common in the Kujavian barrows as to be regarded as deliberate, with the mounds laid out asymmetrically from the start. Indeed, looking along the mound from its narrow end, it gives a very strong impression of being longer and wider than it really is.

This is not a feature that has been sufficiently considered in the analysis of the construction and design of monuments. However, in their recent discussion of the Neolithic long mounds from along the Atlantic façade at Prissé-la-Charrière, Le Manio II and several other sites, Laporte *et al.* (2002, Fig. 5.4) have commented on precisely the same characteristic – the explicit asymmetry of the mounds, with the eastern façades being offset from the principal axis. They have suggested that this was conceived at the planning stage of the monument and that it may relate to the positioning of the entrances to the chambers. While such an interpretation works well for Prissé-la-Charrière and for Barnanez, for example, it does not of course explain the asymmetry present in the long mounds in which the chambers were not really accessible from the long sides.

These patterns, evident on so many sites, suggest that the monument builders were deliberately using simple elements of perspective to create an impression of even more imposing size. As Laporte *et al.* remind us, the use of such perspective is well known from the stone alignments at Carnac, where the size and the varied spacing of the standing stones has been used in conjunction with the lay of the land to create the illusion of shorter or longer distances. We may thus assume that impressions created by approaching or departing from the long mounds were significant. In the case of the earthen long barrow cemeteries it is clear from the number of interred individuals that the actual burial ceremonies were few and far between, but the sites would also have provided a focus for activities of a commemorative nature.

Indeed, the graves within the long barrows, usually placed along the central axis of the monument, take up only a very small amount of interior space, and there is ample evidence that other activities – either directly related to burial ceremonies or of a more general nature – were taking place at various stages of the use of the monuments.

There are traces of small buildings, internal partitions and other features that indicate that pre- and post-funerary ceremonies were performed within the monuments. Internal divisions are known from many Western Pomeranian and Danish barrows (Midgley 1985). These take the form of low transverse stone walls or timber fences, creating small spaces either separating individual graves (for example at Karsko or Østergård) or dividing the interior of the mound into numerous segments; the Barkær long barrows offering an ultimate example of such partitioning.

The cemetery at Escolives-Sainte-Camille brought to light features which confirm that the interior may have had separate sacred areas devoted to different

1 Danubian long house from Bylany prior to excavation. *With permission from Bylany Archive, Institute of Archaeology, Prague*

2 Reconstruction of a Danubian long house built at the archaeological experimental centre at Louny, Bohemia. *Magdalena S. Midgley*

3 An assortment of Danubian ceramics from Bylany, Bohemia. *Magdalena S. Midgley*

4 Typical examples of TRB material culture. *Jażdżewski 1981*

5 TRB axe hoard from Hagelbjerggård. *Copyright National Museum of Denmark, Copenhagen*

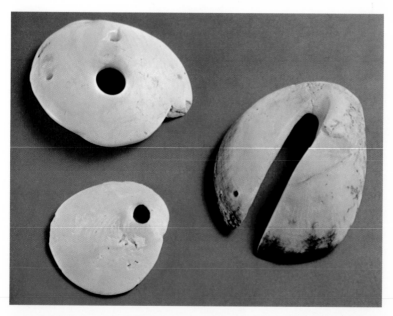

6 Above Reconstruction of
a double burial from
Téviec. *With kind permission
of Serge Cassen*

7 Left Spondylus shells
from the Nitra cemetery,
Slovakia. *Pavúk 1981*

8 Opposite Marble beads
from grave 9/88 at
Vedrovice. *Podborský et al.
2003, with kind permission of
Prof. Podborský*

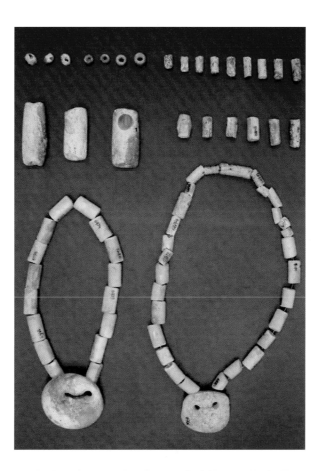

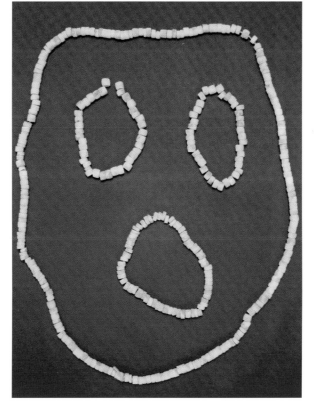

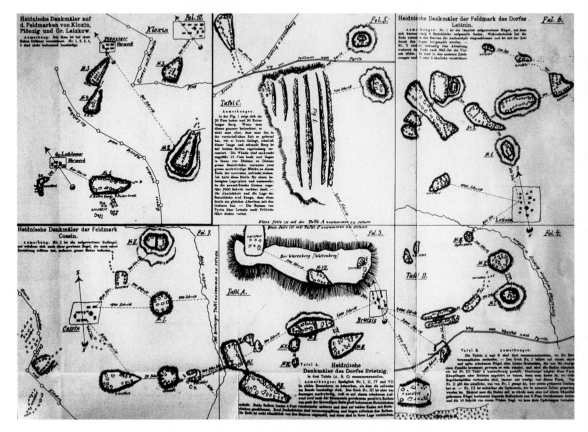

9 Long barrow cemeteries from Western Pomerania surveyed in 1825 by von Plön. *Holsten and Zahnow 1920*

Opposite

10 *Above* Long barrow cemetery of Escolives-Sainte-Camille in the process of excavation. *Magdalena S. Midgley*

11 *Below* Cemetery of La Jardelle. Monument A – superimposition of a circular monument upon a long mound. *Excavation: J.-P. Pautreau, aerial photograph A. Ollivier reproduced with kind permission of J.-P. Pautreau*

12 Opposite above Professor T. Wiślański by the long barrow at Karsko, Western Pomeranian. *Magdalena S. Midgley*

13 Opposite below Excavation of a timber chamber from monument D at Escolives-Sainte-Camille. *Magdalena S. Midgley*

14 Above Escolives-Sainte-Camille with *'fer à cheval'* partitions within the interior of monuments. *Magdalena S. Midgley*

15 *Above* Stone cist from mound B at La Jardelle. *Excavation and photograph J.-P. Pautreau, with kind permission*

Opposite from top

16 Double burial from Escolives-Sainte-Camille. *Magdalena S. Midgley*

17 Green stone neck pendant and four transverse arrowheads from a grave (feature no.100) at Escolives-Sainte-Camille. *Magdalena S. Midgley*

18 Excavation of a cattle skull deposited in one of the pits of monument H at Escolives-Sainte-Camille. *Magdalena S. Midgley*

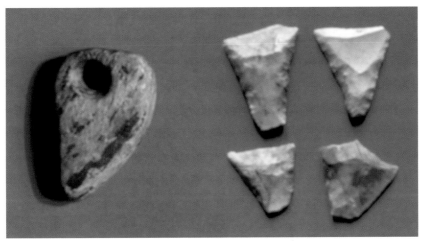

19 Above Square-mouthed vessel from Passy. *Copyright Sens Museum*

20 Opposite 'Eiffel Tower' bone spatulas from the cemetery at Passy. *Copyright Sens Museum*

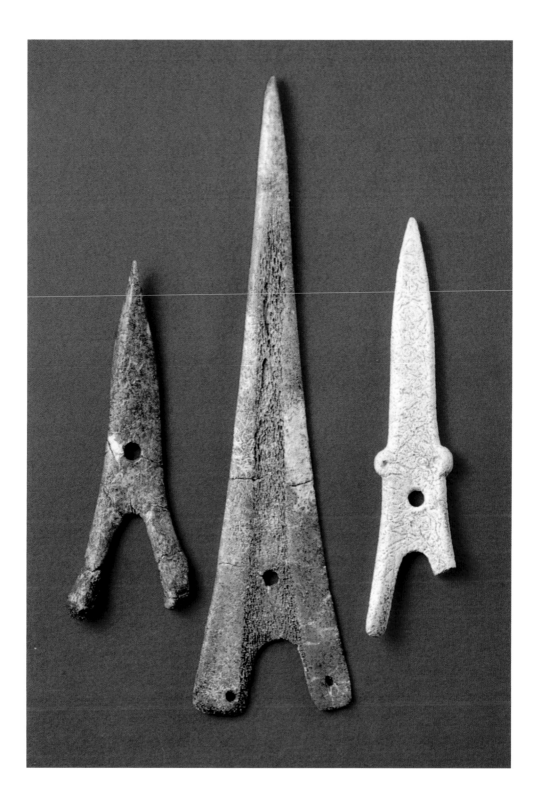

21 Above Mike Ilett by the ruins of the destroyed long house reconstructed by Claude Constantin in 1997. *Magdalena S. Midgley*

22 Opposite Bożejewice: superimposition of a Lengyel house upon an earlier LBK house. *Cerniak 1998*

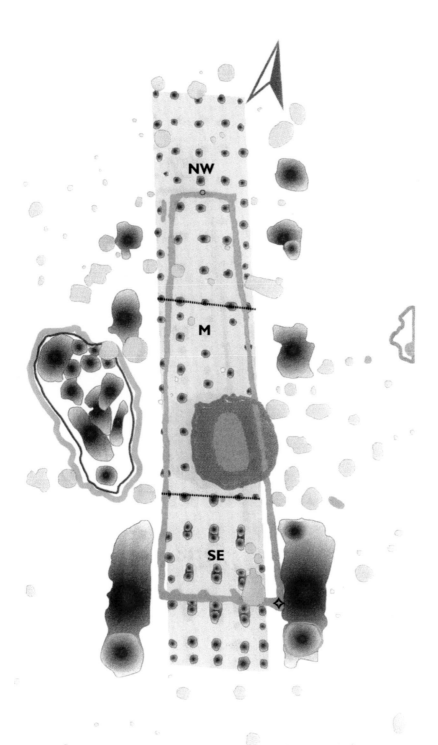

NW

M

SE

10 m

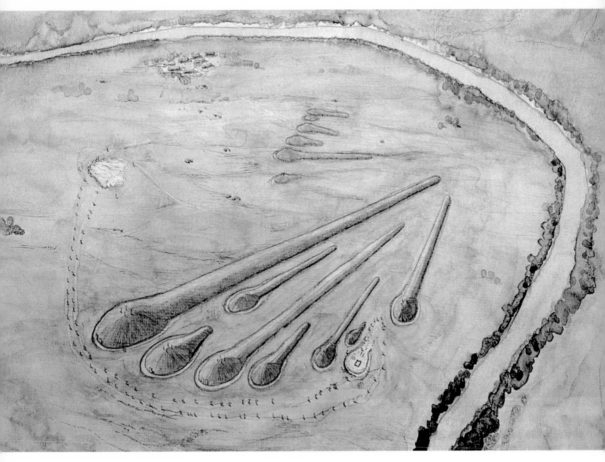

23 An artist's vision of the monumental long barrow cemetery of Passy, watercolour by Jean-Claude Golvin.
Reproduced with kind permission of Éditions Errance, Paris

activities. At least three of the excavated barrows revealed the so-called *fer à cheval* – curious, horse-shoe-shaped arrangements of ditch segments (*24* and *colour plate 14*). The one within monument E, to the west of a series of several grave pits, yielded traces of individual timber posts, although a similar feature within monument F was extremely shallow and post traces could not be observed. Two massive pits joined by a shallow trench were noted at the eastern end of monument D, and a similar arrangement, albeit on a reduced scale, was replicated at the western end. The pits may well have held large posts, perhaps linked to each other with timber planks, creating a sort of 'internal' façade or screen.

These arrangements were important in the creation of separate spaces within the confines of a single monument: the area of the graves being clearly separated from that where no graves were to be placed. The latter may have been important in the pre- and post-funerary ceremonies which had to be performed within the monument itself but nevertheless kept separate from the immediate vicinity of the graves. The structures in barrow D at Escolives-Sainte-Camille strongly suggest that funerary processions may have taken place between the two timber façades: perhaps with the body arriving at the wider eastern end and making its way all round the interior of the monument before being committed to the grave.

Movement on the outside and in the interior of an elongated space is, however, different from that which would have been appropriate to a circular space. The latter is interestingly suggested by the structure of monument H (*24*). Here a series of about a dozen individual pits have been arranged in a circle around the central grave pit. Some of the pits contained deposits: one had a cattle skull, another was full of very dark burnt organic material. In contrast to others, this monument offers a much more open-plan structure, which may have involved circulating around individual standing posts.

Generally, there are no structures obstructing the entrance to the interior of the monuments, although several of the Passy barrows, for example numbers 8, 5 and 15 (Duhamel 1997, Fig. 30a) had timber posts placed in a row in front of the entrance. The row of posts discovered parallel to one of the barrows at Fleury-sur-Orne may be a vestige of a similar post arrangement. Several barrows at Balloy also reveal traces of individual post holes at entrances, for example numbers X, XI and IX had a curious separate cavity at the centre of the entrance to the monument; the presence of about 100kg of sandstone fragments within it has been interpreted as the possible remains of a standing stone (Mordant 1997, 454).

While there is little indication of the precise nature of these structures, it is not inconceivable that post holes in front of the eastern ends of the barrows, or the eastern timber façades known from Denmark, held large decorated timber posts, in the manner of the totem poles familiar from ethnographic accounts. Indeed, the menhirs set on top or in the vicinity of megalithic tombs, known

in such profusion along the Atlantic seaboard, may well have had their counterparts in perishable materials; alas, such 'timber menhirs' dug into the tops of
the long barrow mounds would hardly have survived. They may have been
similarly decorated, with images of axes, cattle bucrania, stylised anthropomorphic and zoomorphic images etc., and may have functioned as totemic markers,
associating individual monuments with a specific family or community group.

Some French barrows also have traces of interior buildings. A U-shaped
ground plan was found inside monument D at Escolives-Sainte-Camille and
similar structures were noted by Henri Carré at Passy. Indeed, a couple of
open-ended stone structures – one U-shaped and one oval – has also been
reported in association with grave chambers at one of the Łupawa barrows
(Jankowska 1999). Such structures may be plausibly interpreted as open-ended
ceremonial buildings, perhaps similar in form and function to the later
Scandinavian cult houses of the Ferslev and Tustrup type, although the latter
were located outwith the actual burial monuments. Bodies may have been
displayed here before the actual burial took place or food offerings collected
prior to a funeral feast; unfortunately there are no finds associated with these
buildings so their interpretation remains conjectural.

Small timber buildings are known from the Kujavian barrows, for example
at Gaj, Obałki or Zberzyn, where they tend to be located at the wider, eastern
end (Midgley 1985, 148-52). There was a clear gap in the stone kerb allowing
access to the buildings directly from the outside, but it seems unlikely that one
could pass further into the interior of the monuments. The fact that several of
these buildings seem to have smouldered very slowly under the earthen mound
suggests that they may have functioned as temples for use after the burial ceremonies – when graves could no longer be accessed – and were burnt down
when no longer required.

The presence of all these structures, while they differ from one region to the
next in specific details, does therefore suggest that monumental long barrow
cemeteries were also places for ceremonies other than burials. These may have
involved visitations to enable spiritual communication with the dead, offer
libations appeasing the ancestral spirits, perform ritual acts in remembrance of
those interred inside or, on a broader level, perhaps involve the *rites de passage*
at significant stages of an individual's life.

CHAPTER 5

LONG BARROWS: GRAVES AND BURIALS

GRAVE FORMS

In contrast to previous assumptions of the simplicity of graves in the long barrows, it now seems that many must have been quite elaborate timber or timber-and-stone structures, some even retaining access to the interior for sufficiently long periods to enable further interments. The most convincing evidence for such graves is to be found in French cemeteries, as well as among the long mounds in Denmark. It was in fact the Danish excavations, from the mid-1960s and throughout the 1970s, that demonstrated that the continental long mounds were anything but 'chamberless' (Madsen 1979 and literature therein). This permitted a reassessment of older excavations whose grave features were not always properly understood, and provided experience to be applied to the interpretation of similar remains from other regions.[*]

A majority of the long barrow graves were constructed within grave pits, although some were placed directly on the old land surface. They display a remarkable variety of construction: pits lined with timber planks, or occasion-ally with thin stone slabs, are prevalent in France. Rectangular chambers made of timber planks, supported within an external stone frame and often covered by a mantle of stones, are typically encountered in the Kujavian, Western Pomeranian and Moravian cemeteries, as well as in Denmark; the little stone cairns regularly tumbling into the grave upon the decay of the timber roof. In other instances the bodies, either in a coffin or wrapped in a shroud, were simply placed in the grave pit.

[*]Detailed descriptions of the Danish chambers may be found in Midgley 1985, and in 1992 Liversage provided a further update on the subject.

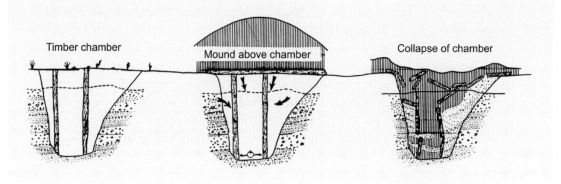

| Timber chamber | Mound above chamber | Collapse of chamber |

30 Reconstruction of timber grave chamber from barrow 15 at Passy. *Duhamel 1997*

The grave pits may be quite large, up to 3m in length, 1.5m wide and 1.2m deep, usually with vertical side walls. The grave fills are homogeneous materials different from the underlying substratum. In some instances they contain particles of charcoal, tiny flint flakes and fragmented potsherds, suggesting that the soil piled up directly over the graves may well have derived from previous occupation surfaces; at other times these are soils intentionally collected from watery environments. The reconstruction of grave 1 from barrow 15 at Passy, based on the analysis of its cross-section, suggests a massive chamber of timber planks constructed inside the pit. When the timber roof finally collapsed, the earth from the mound above it fell *en masse* into the void below (*30*).

At Escolives-Sainte-Camille, a grave pit inside monument D, unfortunately surviving only in its southern half, revealed a cross-section identical to that described from Passy, with the dark staining of the timber wall still visible (*colour plate 13*). The fill of the grave pit in monument G tells a similar story. Apart from planks, wooden stakes may also have been used to line the graves; the oval outline of dark staining following the inner walls of the central pit in monument C suggests that timber posts were hammered in along its edges to create a fairly sturdy chamber. In the case of such chambers, built deeply into a pit, access to the interior must undoubtedly have been from above.

With rare exceptions, the graves from the Kujavian and Western Pomeranian barrows have not been subject to excavations meticulous enough to reveal such details. Nevertheless, as I have suggested before (Midgley 1985), many of the Kujavian graves can also be seen as complex structures employing timber and stone in their constructions. Wooden chambers, built either within relatively shallow pits or directly on the old land surface, were surrounded at ground level by a low, stone, rectangular setting usually of one, rarely of more courses. Naturally, the timber elements have not survived within the acidic soils, but the perfectly regular shapes of the stone setting make it absolutely clear that they rested against a straight and solid wall; examples of such graves are known from several barrows at Sarnowo, Obałki, Leśniczówka, Wietrzychowice and Zberzyn (Midgley 1985, Figs. 61, 62, 64, 66).

In addition, the central grave at Wietrzychowice may even have had access to the interior on the ground level, as the western wall of the surrounding stone enclosure had a wide gap in it. Such chambers were often protected with a little stone cairn but clearly protruded above it, as the gap in the stones corresponds in size and shape to the chamber below. Similar chambers have also been recorded among the individual long mounds of Mecklenburg, with those at Güstrow, Gnewitz and Rothenmoor providing textbook examples of this type (Midgley 1985, Fig. 63).

Apart from timber-built chambers, some long mounds have graves constructed principally in stone. The cemeteries of La Jardelle, Rots and Fleury-sur-Orne provide interesting examples of such stone-built chambers. At La Jardelle there was a slightly trapezoidal structure built of vertically placed slabs within an oval pit, covered with two additional slabs (*31* and *colour plate 15*). At Rots, 135 thin limestone slabs (altogether over one tonne in weight) were used in the construction of the western chamber in monument 3: three large slabs covered the pit floor while smaller ones were

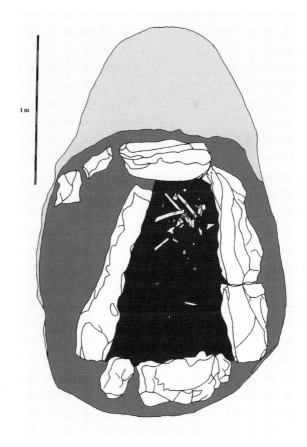

31 Stone cist from mound B at La Jardelle. *Excavation: J.-P. Pautreau, drawing by V. Marluz with kind permission of J.-P. Pautreau*

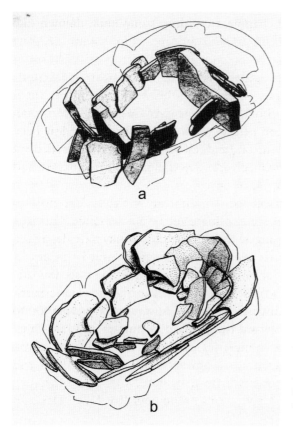

32 Stone chambers from long barrow cemetery at Rots: a) Monument 2 chamber 1; b) Monument 3 chamber 1. *Desloges 1997*

placed vertically along the edges of the pit, overlapping one another and with their rugged edges to the bottom. A timber roof was also covered with slabs, which tumbled into the interior upon its collapse. In monument 2 the pit floor was also paved and two large slabs were placed upright in the manner of orthostats. The covering consisted of four large, flat pieces of limestone which must have rested on a central perishable support: a block of timber resting within little notches cut into the two orthostats (*32*).

The close morphological relationship between such stone- and timber-built chambers is most clearly expressed in the westerly grave in the southern barrow at Barkær, which is a stone replica of the neighbouring timber chamber. In Liversage's words, 'It would be hard to find stones that more faithfully reproduced the shape of large crudely split planks' (Liversage 1992, 22, Figs. 10-12). Many other Danish barrows reveal similar associations between timber- and stone-built graves: Tolstrup, Troelstrup, Skibshøj, Mosegården, Bygholm Nørremark and Lindebjerg are the most obvious examples (Madsen 1979; Midgley 1985), and the timber graves are not invariably the earliest. The Skibshøj chamber was, in fact, a hybrid structure, with the inner side walls constructed of uprights with dry-stone walling on top of them and five wooden planks resting atop in the form of a roof (Jørgensen 1977). The long barrow

LA 3 at Flintbek had three timber chambers and three stone-built, dolmen-like chambers, in addition to two possible graves with tree-trunk coffins (*28*; *Zich* 1993, 23 and 25).

Apart from timber chambers, stone cists were also built in Western Pomeranian barrows, for example at Łupawa (the excavator called them 'dolmens'; Jankowska 1999, 217). Stone and timber were also used in Moravian cemeteries. While the cross section of a grave from Otaslavice, published by Šmíd (2000, Fig. 3) is rather schematic, it does indicate a vertical-walled pit with a roof of flat slabs; it is not inconceivable that the pit was timber-lined and the slabs rested on a timber roof of some sort.

Reconstructing timber chambers from such scanty traces does not, of course, permit greater detail, yet we may assume they were elaborate. Carvings from later 'megalithic' chambers suggest that similar motifs may have decorated the inner and outer walls – either painted or carved in wood. Images of bucrania, motifs familiar to us from pottery and carvings of axes, so dramatically preserved on megalith walls, may well have had their organic counterparts.

Apart from these variously constructed chambers, some of the dead found within the confines of the long barrows were buried in simpler ways, as not all grave pits from the monumental cemeteries display evidence of structures. Such, for example, is the interpretation of some of the graves from Rots and Fleury-sur-Orne, although without any firm inner framework it is difficult to account for the regularity of grave pit 2 from monument 2 at Rots (Desloges 1997, Fig. 8).

The two individuals for whom barrow 8 at Sarnowo appears to have been extended were put in to the grave pits in narrow wooden coffins (the pits not exceeding 75cm in their maximum width; Midgley 1985, Fig. 65). The coffins were identified by perfectly rectangular, narrow bands of a white, chalky substance, and it is not inconceivable that they were painted; a timber coffin has equally been suggested for the individual buried in barrow 9 (*ibid.* Fig. 67). We have already noted the two tree-trunk coffins from Flintbek; a wooden coffin was lowered into the grave pit at Bjørnsholm; and it is reasonable to interpret some of the shallow, narrow and regular grave pits from the barrows at Sachsenwald as possible examples of coffin burials. Chambon, analysing the skeletal remains from the long barrow cemeteries at Passy, Balloy and other French Neolithic burials, has argued that the decomposition of some bodies suggests a small, confined but not in-filled space of the sort entirely in keeping with the use of coffins (Chambon 1997, 2003).

It is also worth noting at this point that burial chambers – in timber or in stone – need not be confined to long mounds only. Excavations of a number of the so-called flat cemeteries of the TRB culture, most notably in Schleswig-Holstein but also known from other areas (sometimes in the vicinity of the long barrows – for example at Sarnowo or Malice Kościelne in Poland), suggest that timber chambers were common burial structures, whether covered by a mound or not. Indeed at the French cemetery of Orville, on the Plaine de Beauce, graves were covered by stone slabs, either resting on stone walls or on the edges of pits; of these the best known is the impressive grave of Malesherbes (Simonin *et al.* 1997). At Vignely, Seine-et-Marne, where Cerny burials have been found, several graves appear to correspond to those from Balloy (Chambon and Lanchon 2001) and, as a further example, we may note a row of three pit graves from Antran, Vienne, each paved in stone with timber walls and roofs (Pautreau 1991). In Denmark, the numerous so-called earth graves (*jordgrav*) – known since the nineteenth century – also fit into this category, although many of them most likely belonged within the long, ploughed-out barrows.

FROM TIMBER TO STONE

While the majority of graves contain a single individual, there are, neverthe-less, examples of multiple burials. Thus the question arises as to how such practices should be interpreted: were these simultaneous depositions of several individuals or were the chambers reopened to admit subsequent interments at a later stage? Indeed, are we seeing the beginning of collective burial practices witnessed in many megaliths?

The long barrow chambers constructed of stone slabs were, theoretically at least, permanent structures that could be used to house subsequent interments if required. The slab-built chamber B at La Jardelle, in fact, contained remains of a single individual, but the somewhat later grave in barrow C had remains of about 20 individuals; apart from the six earliest interments of three adults, two children and a neonate, the others were regularly moved and rearranged in order to accommodate new burials (Pautreau *et al.* 2003, 48).

Timber-built chambers present a somewhat different case. On the one hand, access is related to the survival of timber itself and, on the other hand, to the treatment of the chamber – covering it with a mound of earth makes it less likely that it would be reopened later. It is generally assumed that such graves, irrespective of the number of individuals involved, were designed for one burial ceremony. However, while not frequent, multiple burials within timber-built chambers are known.

At Bygholm Nørremark, four adults were laid in a timber grave, although the arrangement of the bodies – in opposing pairs – suggests a single act of burial. Similar interments are suggested at some French barrows: for example the child and adult at Passy (grave 17.3), and the two children and the two adults at Gron (graves 356 and 360). On the other hand, superposition of one body upon the other – involving either children or an adult and a child – is known from Balloy and from Passy; the sediments covering the earliest burial suggest that some time had elapsed before the second individual was interred up above and that the chamber must have remained visible above ground over that period.

However, a recently excavated grave from Escolives-Sainte-Camille (*colour plate 16*) shows unequivocally that timber chambers could remain accessible for some time. This chamber was closed, presumably with a wooden roof, after the first individual was buried. Sufficient time elapsed for the first body to have decomposed before it was reopened, and the skeletal remains were moved aside to accommodate the body of the second individual (Duhamel and Midgley forthcoming).

To what extent this sort of double interment constitutes the beginning of collective burial is a matter for future consideration. We have already observed such a pattern in some late Mesolithic cemeteries, most notably at Téviec and Hoëdic where the little stone cists were sometimes reopened to accept additional bodies (for example, graves C and F at Hoëdic and grave K at Téviec), or where the location of a grave seems to have been remembered (for example at Varennes). However, with the chambers in long barrows we should think in terms of a conscious decision to leave them accessible for some time: the double grave at Escolives-Sainte-Camille demonstrates that no mound was piled up on top of the chamber prior to the second interment.

There are, of course, profound differences between the truly collective graves, such as the later *allées couvertes* of the Paris Basin (Masset and Soulier 1995) or the so-called *Mauerkammer* chambers constructed in the later TRB in parts of central and northern Germany (Müller 2001), some of which contained the remains of over 200 individuals. Nevertheless, the principle of accessibility of timber-built burial chamber has been established, and this practice was an important feature of the burial tradition within the long barrow cemeteries.

This has important implications for our understanding of the relationship between the long barrow graves and the subsequent development of the megalithic stone chambers; while the earliest dolmen forms may still have been intended for individual burials, the majority of stone chambers whose interiors were accessible provide evidence for multiple burials. The idea of a unilinear evolutionary development of different chamber forms along the Atlantic façade from simple cists to passage graves, which characterised the Breton megalithic research for more than a century, is now being eschewed in favour of contemporaneity of different forms deriving from the diversity of cultural influences converging in Brittany from the beginning of the fifth millennium BC onwards (Boujot and Cassen 1993; Laporte and Joussaume 2003). Indeed, in the Paris Basin, the timber-built chambers in the long barrows can be juxtaposed with other forms of Cerny graves, such as the pit graves covered with large stone slabs (*sépultures sous dalle*) known from Malesherbes and Auneau (Simonin *et al.* 1997; Verjux 2002). The chronological parameters of these different forms still remain to be established more precisely, but the presence of different forms of complex burial structures is significant.

However, as far as the North European Plain is concerned, the timber-built graves within the long barrows belong, on present evidence, to the earliest horizon and represent the first manifestations of burial chambers in the region, beginning in Kujavia at about 4400 BC. The earliest dolmens contain pottery belonging to the so-called Fuchsberg horizon, which cannot be dated to before 3700 BC. Thus, while in the west of Europe we can recognise the multiplicity of early monumental burial structures, the process in the north seems to have followed a different course. While unilinear 'evolutionary' development schemes are not fashionable in current archaeological interpretations, there is nothing in the archaeological record of this region to contradict the suggestion that the earliest stone-built chambers, the so-called *Urdolmen*, must be seen as stone replicas of the already popular timber versions. The entire north European sequence – from the *Urdolmen* to the passage grave – seems to be rooted in the tradition of elaborate timber chambers, which had already been constructed for several centuries within the long mounds.

LOCATION OF GRAVES WITHIN OLD HOUSES

In our discussion of the location of barrows we have already noted that many of the cemeteries, as well as individual monuments, were erected on previously settled areas. This relationship appears to be even closer in some instances, because it involves intentional construction of the graves within the disused house foundations. The cultural superimpositions are, however, complex. In the Yonne and Seine river valleys the monumental cemeteries are placed on or close to the late Danubian sites, which by then appear to have been abandoned.

That this pattern is not exclusive to western Europe is borne out in the location of the two long burial structures at Březno, about 300m away from a concentration of *Stichbandkeramik* houses (Pleinerová 1971, 39). Curiously enough, the late Danubian settlement in the area of Kujavia – and possibly in other selected enclaves across the southern fringes of the North European Plain – is contemporary with the earliest manifestations of the TRB culture. On present evidence, the cemeteries in this vast area, as well as in southern Scandinavia, are built upon the early abandoned TRB sites. The implications of this will be made clear later.

The deliberate intent behind such choice of locations can hardly be questioned. It is inconceivable that those who came to bury the individuals placed in monuments XV and XVI at Balloy were not aware that they were burying them within the dilapidated foundations of earlier houses (*33*). While the cemetery at Passy was located near the older Danubian settlement, vestiges of which were most likely visible on the surface, as well as the contemporary Cerny sites, there is no evidence that any of the barrows intentionally overlaid domestic structures.

At Gron *Les Sablons*, Yonne, two monuments were constructed about 60m to the north of the earlier Danubian village. The central grave of monument 1

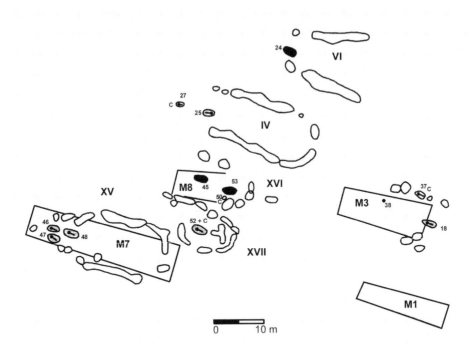

33 Balloy – central part of the cemetery demonstrating the superimposition of the Cerny graves and long barrows upon the Villeneuve-Saint-Germain houses. *Mordant 1997*

was located in an area of about 50 post holes indicative of some earlier structures. Their pattern is neither suggestive of a Danubian long house nor does it conform to any Cerny-type house, and yet it is clear that some sort of construction was there before the area became devoted to burials; we cannot say whether those involved in the burial activities were aware of what was there earlier (Müller *et al.* 1997, Figs 3 and 4).

In Kujavia, the celebrated site of Sarnowo provides by far the clearest evidence. Here the old land surface from underneath the mounds revealed traces of the very early TRB settlement: hearths, rubbish pits, broken pottery, animal bones etc. Irrespective of the controversy over the plough-marks, it is clear that the central grave in barrow 8 cut through an earlier house: traces of clay floor, fragments of daub, post holes along the walls, and large amounts of typical cultural debris leave little doubt as to the visibility and domestic function of that structure.

Other Kujavian cemeteries were similarly placed, although the evidence is often ambiguous. Against the background of current knowledge, some of the ritual 'hearth-middens' found under the mounds would today be more appropriately interpreted as occupational debris than as the remains of funerary feastings. The evidence from Les'niczówka, however, makes it hard to dismiss the idea of funerary feasts altogether, since the 'hearth-middens' here are above the graves. Indeed, Jażdżewski commented on the strength of some of these fires and their effect upon the boulders of the stone kerb (Jażdżewski 1936, 174).

Evidence from Denmark is perhaps best known in the literature, and the placement upon abandoned TRB settlements is characteristic of many Danish long barrows. Indeed the original, if misguided, interpretation by Glob of the two long barrows from Barkær as being remains of 'Danubian-style' long houses is only partly attributable to the similarity between long-barrow and long-house forms; the presence of domestic debris found scattered everywhere made his 1949 interpretation perfectly acceptable.

A few further examples will suffice: the placement of the grave chamber within the foundations of an older TRB house at Bjørnsholm has already been mentioned and, against this background, the central grave from Bygholm Nørremark can be confidently interpreted in the same way. Other graves located directly on settlements include Konens Høj, Stengade (as controversial as Barkær), Lindebjerg. Mosegården, Rustrup and Tolstrup – all clearly demonstrating an intentional relationship between graves and settlements.

HUMAN REMAINS

Human remains recovered from the long barrows are generally poorly preserved and in many graves there are simply no remains, although the grave goods do suggest that a body was once present. Moreover, there is little information on possible burials inserted into the mounds and on those which might have been placed in the immediate vicinity, but nevertheless outwith the monuments. At Balloy, about ten largely eroded graves were found outside the barrows and a further five within the actual ditches defining the monuments (Mordant 1997, 461; Chambon 1997, 489). At Sarnowo, about 50m northwest from the nearest long barrow, remains of 17 persons were found; these are generally considered to be settlement burials, but the close spatial relation to the cemetery is significant.

Similarly, at Malice Kościelne, at least ten graves were placed immediately to the east of the long mound. The mound itself is problematic: the excavators have suggested a rather wide barrow with at least three longitudinal rows of stones in the interior, with numerous burials either side of the northern 'inner' row (Bargieł *et al.* 1998, Fig. 2). A different interpretation might suggest two separate mounds and then half of these internal burials would, in effect, be outside the barrow itself.

Where human remains do survive they reveal that the dead were buried fully articulated, laid out in an extended position, on their back with arms stretched out along the sides of the body – a tradition that dates deeply into the preceding Mesolithic. This practice is witnessed everywhere and, where the bodies have totally decayed, it finds further support in the size of the burial chambers and the disposition of grave goods.

Nevertheless, exceptions to this appear everywhere. At Passy, at least eight individuals were placed with arms and legs flexed to varying degrees, and one of these (grave 2 in barrow 11) was even described by Duhamel as in a 'classic Danubian' position (Duhamel 1997, 414). Of the bodies buried at Balloy at least six had their extremities flexed to various degrees, and those buried at Rots were placed in a crouched position.

Scanty though it is, all evidence from the Kujavian cemeteries also points to a typical extended inhumation, and the slight deviations in the position of arms or legs seem to be related to decomposition of the corpse. Chambon discussed this issue in great detail in his analysis of the skeletons from Balloy (Chambon 1997). The human remains from other areas – this regrettably includes Denmark and north Germany – are so scanty that any generalisations are not justified; we should, however, note that the size of the burial chambers does indicate that the dead were buried, as elsewhere, primarily in an extended position.

While inhumation is without any doubt the principal form of disposal of the dead in the long barrows, cremations have been noted as well. Šmíd comments on the apparent sequence of burials within the Moravian long barrows where the early Baalberge phase is characterised by inhumations, to be replaced by cremations in the later phases (Šmíd 2003, 104). Only one cremation is reported from Balloy and Duhamel noted three instances of child cremation at Passy (Duhamel 1997, 421 and 425).

Cremation is the only burial rite observed at the Łupawa cemetery (14 individuals in a concentration of over 30 barrows) and no inhumations have come to light so far. The preservation of organic materials in this region is very poor, and even in the neighbouring settlement only small quantities of burnt animal bone survive. It is thus not inconceivable that some individuals were inhumed – there are several grave structures whose size permits extended inhumation – and a double burial rite may have been practised at this somewhat peripheral and rather late cemetery.

AGE AND SEX

Due to the vagaries of preservation, the overall number of individuals buried in cemeteries is difficult to estimate: 45 skeletons survived at Balloy, 30 at Passy, and so far the remains of six individuals have been recovered at Escolives-Sainte-Camille. In Kujavia nine skeletons survived at Sarnowo, six at Wietrzychowice, while other sites have yielded altogether only one or two remains.

These figures are, naturally, unhelpful to any discussion of demographic issues, be it in terms of group size, rates of mortality etc. They do, however, show beyond any doubt that only a tiny minority of individuals in each community were given such an impressive placement in death. Indeed, even in cases where no human remains survive, the number of graves in individual monuments across the whole of their distribution bears this out.

What has become equally clear from anthropological analyses is that both sexes and all ages – from newborn babies to mature adults – were buried in the barrows. While there were no children either at Sarnowo or at Wietrzychowice, a burial of a three-year-old child was found in one of the barrows at Leśniczówka. Jażdżewski considered this a 'sacrifice' but, against the background of present knowledge, this is an unlikely interpretation. Of the 30 individuals at Passy at least 11 were children (three were babies), while 14 children were definitely identified at Balloy. At both cemeteries there seems to be a dearth of teenagers: apparently no one aged between 10 and 17 years was buried at Balloy, and only one child at Passy was 12 to 14 years of age. Irrespective of the problems identified earlier, the data from Malice Kościelne are interesting. The eight individuals buried to the south of the northern 'inner wall' included five children aged between two and four years old, and altogether children accounted for more than half of the individuals buried at that site (Kozak-Zychman and Gauda 1998).

We already considered the pitfalls of sexing individuals using human skeletal remains and the even greater difficulties in determining this on the basis of grave goods (chapter 3), and these problems apply equally to the dead from the long barrows. Only two individuals at Passy were identified as young females. Balloy skeletons were better preserved and, among the adults, there were 11 males and 12 females, but children's skeletons could not be sexed. Of the six individuals buried at Gron, four were adult males (one mature) and two were children. Children as well as adults were also buried at La Jardelle. The available anthropological analyses from Kujavia are quite old but there is no reason to assume they are wrong. At Sarnowo there were six adult males and three women (one mature and two of about 18 years old), and of the six adults at Wietrzychowice four were identified as males (two in their 30s and two about 50). We shall return to the significance of these sex and age aspects in due course.

RITUAL TREATMENT OF BODIES

There is little evidence for the treatment of the bodies prior to burial. Perhaps the most dramatic change from the preceding Mesolithic and Danubian burial practices is the truly dramatic reduction in the use of ochre. Only very occasionally is there any evidence either for the use of ochre on the bodies or for substances similar to ochre. Possible nodules of ochre deposited in the graves have been noted in the French cemeteries: once at Gron, once at Passy, twice at Balloy and Rots. But only one skeleton, at Passy, seems to have been sprinkled with this substance (Passy 4.1, see below). The Kujavian cemeteries similarly reveal no evidence of its use, although some of the dead at Sarnowo seem to have been covered with a white, calcareous substance, possibly a residue from layers of shells. A beaker from Lindebjerg contained some traces of ochre (Liversage 1981, 117), and the two end stones of one of the Stengade graves had a mineral crust with ochre contents on them. In the latter case the excavator thought ochre was used in the burial ceremony but the two crusts were the only traces (Skaarup 1975b, 30). Recently, Strassburg has commented on several additional south Scandinavian long barrow burials in which ochre may have played a role (Strassburg 2000, 357-58), but these are sporadic rather than regular occurrences.

There is equally little evidence for the manipulation of the remains of the dead. The skeletons from the French cemeteries seem to have been placed in graves intact. The presence of cremations (one at Balloy and three at Passy) has tentatively raised the question of sacrificial rites accompanying proper burials, but the evidence is ambiguous and, at this stage, the issue must remain open.

Two individuals buried at barrow 8 at Sarnowo revealed posthumous breakages of their long bones, which were interpreted as possible indications of a burial ritual involving cannibalism. In this context we may consider the complete as well as partial remains of the dead found within the confines of the Sarnowo settlement. Osteological analysis of the bones revealed differences in treatment between these and the remains recovered from the long barrows. The settlement burials showed distinctive traces of burning – not classic cremations, but rather charring of the bodies at fairly low temperatures between 100 and 180 degrees centigrade prior to or during the burial ceremonies. Some of the skulls, however, were subject to much higher temperatures and, together with their associated breakages, have been interpreted as indicative of ritual cannibalism. Similarly treated assemblages of human bones were apparently recovered from within the mound of barrow 7, but no further analyses are available.

GRAVE GOODS

On the whole the grave goods placed with the dead in the long barrows are scanty, although the French and Danish burials tend to be more richly equipped than those in other areas. In general a ceramic pot or two, flint tools and jewellery are among the common grave furnishings: some individuals wore necklaces of wild animal teeth, shell and, in the more northerly latitudes, amber beads. Rare finds of copper beads and rings in northern Europe suggest that metals, while still immensely exotic, were making their way northwards from the central European production centres.

Before we consider the assortment of goods that were placed with the dead in the long barrows, it is perhaps worth devoting a few words to what constitutes grave goods and how items discovered with the deceased might be regarded.

Archaeologists distinguish, firstly, personal items – objects such as clothing and jewellery – which undoubtedly belonged to the deceased and which, while found in a funerary context, will reflect aspects of daily life. The second category are objects which may or may not reflect daily life but are considered indispensable to the funerary ceremony, be it on account of religious expression, appropriateness as equipment in the afterlife or identification of the status of the deceased. This second category was selected by those performing funerals and reflects specific cultural or regional codes of funerary behaviour.

There is little information on any garments worn by the dead, although occasional finds of beads or shells on atypical parts of the body suggest that they may have been sewn onto garments. Items of jewellery in the French cemeteries include shell and limestone bead necklaces (frequently worn by children), pendants of greenstone rocks (*17*), perforated animal teeth and boars' tusks; less commonly, pieces of mother-of-pearl and scallop shells are found. Jewellery in the burials from the Polish barrows is virtually unknown, although boars' tusks were found near the head of one individual at Sarnowo and at Gaj.

Amber, used in the north throughout the Mesolithic, continues to be fashioned into ornaments in Denmark, and many amber beads – tubular, triangular, disc or figure-of-eight shapes – were found in the graves there. Sometimes they were made into necklaces, and the presence of amber spacers suggests that some comprised several strands; single beads were most likely sewn onto garments and several finds of amber discs, perforated along the edges, are also known. Perforated copper discs have been found in a few Danish barrows. At Rude one was apparently attached to the wrist of the deceased, and similar copper pieces were found at Salten and Konens Høj. The amber discs are without any doubt local replicas of such rare copper ornaments – the colour of amber providing a perfect imitation medium.

Stone and bone tools form another category of grave goods, and here interesting regional differences can be shown. Polished flint axes were a very common accompaniment of the dead in the Danish graves. There can be little doubt that this custom is a continuation of the Mesolithic tradition, when imported Danubian *Schuhleistenkeile* began to be placed with selected dead. Indeed, as we have already seen (chapter 2), the role of the axe within the ritual ceremonial in the TRB culture extends well beyond the funerary sphere.

Once again Kujavia fails to enlighten us in any detail. If bone tools were put into graves they simply have not survived. Rare flint blades and knives were made of imported raw materials; tools made from flint procured through exchanges from the Holy Cross Mountains or Wolhynia might have been significant by virtue of the provenance of the raw materials rather than their function as tools. A stone macehead was discovered in one of the mounds at Wietrzychowice; since it is unlikely that such an item would have been lost, its placement within the body of the mound should be seen as deliberate – alas, such finds are extremely rare.

34 Reconstruction of a burial ceremony at Passy. *Leaflet from the exhibition 'Le Cerny' at the Museum of Prehistory at Nemours*

Many of the graves from the long barrows have also yielded flint arrowheads. While strictly speaking this is correct, there can be little doubt that such finds in effect indicate that arrows regularly accompanied the dead. This could take the form of one or two arrows (for instance at Sarnowo or Bygholm Nørremark) or a larger group (from four overlapping arrowheads at one of the Escolives-Sainte-Camille graves to a bundle of 22 arrows with transverse and triangular tips at Passy; *colour plate 17*). Hunting equipment was thus regularly placed with the dead, be it as a token presence or a quiverful of arrows (*34*). This custom, evidenced everywhere from southern Scandinavia to western France, transcends regional and cultural boundaries to emphasise the importance of hunting across the whole of north-west Europe. We have already alluded briefly to this phenomenon and will return to it later.

Bone tools, on the other hand, survive well in the French cemeteries: various cutting, scraping and polishing tools placed with the dead indicate a wide range and technological expertise in working such raw materials. Sidéra (2000) has suggested that, in comparison with the preceding period, the Cerny culture reflects a real technological evolution as well as an overall increased role of tools made of organic materials in everyday activities. Nevertheless, the symbolic role of these materials – especially the huge boars' tusks fashioned into ornaments – should not be ignored. Indeed, the general indifference to axes as suitable grave goods within the Cerny can hardly be related to the technological and functional role of such implements in everyday life. The very real regional differences across north-west Europe in the ritual significance of tools will be discussed in the final chapter.

In general, pottery was placed with the dead less frequently than was done within the Danubian tradition. In the north it included typical but selected TRB forms: beakers, lugged and collared flasks. No analyses of the contents of such vessels have been conducted and it is therefore not clear what sort of food, if any, they contained. Sherratt has pointed out that an inverted collared flask is '...absurdly like a poppy-head' (Sherratt 1991, 56), and Strassburg commented on its similarity with hallucinatory mushrooms (Strassburg 2000, 398). Soluble opium or other intoxicating substances may well have played an important role in funerary ceremonies: evoking past dead spirits or providing appropriate food for the journey beyond.

Pottery was not common in the French graves but the forms found there are unusual. We have already noted the presence in the Cerny culture of square-mouthed or deliberately 'deformed' vessels (chapter 2; *13* and *colour plate 19*). Three examples have so far been found at Escolives and two at Passy. The Passy vessels are decorated with typical Cerny abstract motifs but one of the Escolives-Sainte-Camille pots had applied decoration in the form of a stylised bucranium under the handle. Such vessels and decoration are common throughout western France, particularly around and to the north of the Loire. The iconographic bovine symbolism represented in these images is further emphasised in the deposition of cattle bucrania in funerary contexts (monument H at Escolives-Sainte-Camille contained a formally placed cattle skull; *colour plate 18*) and, as suggested above, in the possible carved images on the walls of the timber burial chambers.

Just as the exotic copper and amber discs found in the Danish long barrows may have been important symbols defining the status of the deceased, so in the French cemeteries the presence of bone spatulas, described in the literature under the name of 'Eiffel towers', may have performed the same role (*colour plate 20*). These rare bone implements have been found four times at Passy, one uncontexted and three from graves (5.1, 6.1 and 11.1), and one at Balloy. The bone implements from Passy come from unsexed graves, although one is a double grave of an adult and a baby. The Balloy individual accompanied by a spatula, in grave 5, is a male.*

---

*In the table in Mordant 1997 (Fig. 15) this individual is identified as an adult female, elsewhere in the text, however, as male (p. 471); Chambon classifies the individual as male (1997, Fig. 1).

Against the general background of formality and relative poverty of funerary equipment there are, nevertheless, some rather unusual burials within the French cemeteries which stand out on account either of the grave goods or of the burial ritual, and we should consider examples of these.

A young woman of about 20 years of age was buried in barrow 4 at Passy (grave 4.1; Duhamel 1997, 406, Fig. 7). Unusually, the bottom of the grave chamber was strewn with ochre upon which her body was placed in a classic extended position; the body was more to the edge of the grave on its right side, leaving space on the left for the deposition of goods. She wore three pendants on the neck – one made from a fragment of stone bracelet, cut shell and a canine molar – and a fragment of a perforated antler was placed by her head. At the waist, by her left hand, there was a deposit of *Anodon* shells covered with ochre and six bone tools (awls and polishers), two boars' tusks (one perforated) and an assemblage of flint tools including large blades, two flake axes, two knives and a chisel. There were also two pieces of mother-of-pearl and a flint blade, and she held a scallop shell and an oval piece of mother-of-pearl in her left hand. Bernardini has argued that the arrangement and association of these various items suggests that they were placed in soft material containers - a 'tool-bag' with bone implements and another container for the shells, perhaps held together in a still larger container (Bernardini *et al.* 1992). By the right leg she originally must have had a quiver with 12 arrows tipped with transverse and triangular points; there was an antler piece by the left knee as well as two pots by the left leg. It was one of those pots – the richly decorated 'Grossgartach' vessel – that sparked an extraordinary polemic among French archaeologists concerning the chronology and cultural provenance of this single container (Lichardus 1992; Dubouloz 1994; Jeunesse 1995).

The neighbouring monument 5 also contained a richly equipped individual. There was a quiver with 22 arrows (transverse and triangular), a lugged bottle supported the right arm, and by the left side of the head a bone spatula (the 'Eiffel tower') pointed eastwards. The sherds of a square-mouthed vessel were found at the bottom of the grave pit and throughout the fill; most probably the pot stood on the roof of the grave chamber and tumbled down upon its collapse. The central grave from Balloy barrow II seems to belong to the same category. The individual was also distinguished by the presence of a bone spatula, another bone implement, a wild boar's tusk and a canine tooth.

A very different picture emerges from the long barrows on the Plaine de Caen (Desloges 1997). The actual grave goods from Rots and Fleury-sur-Orne are scanty, although an assemblage of 170 small pieces of flint resulting from the manufacture of tools, placed at the bottom of one of the grave pits at Rots, can hardly be accidental. At these sites, however, elements of the late Danubian ritual tradition of providing the dead with meat joints – even complete animals – have continued. Several of the graves yielded only fragments of bones from ovicaprids, but one individual from Fleury had five complete animals placed to the left side of the body; this is more than a symbolic food offering within a pot or, indeed, leftovers from a funerary feast.

SUMMARY

Thus, in summary, the evidence discussed in this chapter reveals that the north-west European long mound graves display a remarkable variety of forms, from simple pit graves to elaborately constructed timber or slab chambers. In many instances access to these structures would have been possible at least for as long as the timber lasted or until the earthen mound sealed the grave; in rare instances, such as at Skibshøj, the actual burial chamber was deliberately set alight. Many of the graves, moreover, show an intimate relationship through spatial position close to or within disused domestic structures. Such patterns are so widespread in north-west Europe that they cannot be regarded as mere accidents or pragmatic uses of previously cleared spaces.

The human remains from long barrows – cemeteries and individual monuments alike – suggest that only a very small proportion of the population were given such a prominent treatment. While in the past this appeared to have been reserved for mature individuals only, the evidence brought to light in recent years has shown that this is not the case; children were equally important when it came to selective burial and this compels us to reconsider some of the past models for TRB and Cerny societies. The grave goods accompanying the dead reflect codes of funerary behaviour which represent both regional and transcendental practices related to social patterns operating in north-west Europe in the middle of the fifth millennium BC, to the disposal of the dead, and to beliefs in the afterlife.

CHAPTER 6

INTERPRETATION OF THE LONG BARROW CEMETERIES

At first glance the long barrow monumental cemeteries signal a dramatic break with the preceding funerary traditions: demonstratively monumental architecture, different burial customs attesting to social transformation and the emergence of new hierarchies within the Neolithic societies of the mid-fifth millennium BC. However, their significance lies not only in these new manifestations, but equally in the encoded symbolism that reflects the merging of the hunter-gatherer and the Danubian worlds.

LOCATION IN THE NATURAL AND CULTURAL LANDSCAPE

While long mounds are found in many regions of continental Europe, we have already noted that the long barrow cemeteries – conglomerations of a dozen or more monuments – display a particular geographical distribution. They are found intermittently upon that vast arc that corresponds to the broad cultural boundary between the north-west European hunter-gatherers and the central European Danubian farmers: from the area of Kujavia in the east to the Paris Basin in the west, a region which was fundamental to the emergence of the TRB and Cerny communities. They are also being recognised in the regions of Bohemia and Moravia – areas which, with the river Danube, form the southern boundary of the territory of the first central European farmers.

Although, on the one hand, we need to consider the long barrow cemeteries on a pan-European scale, it is also evident that regional considerations – cultural as well as natural – played a role, and the regional level of analysis must not be eschewed. Thus the placement of the monuments and the use of different raw materials in the construction of barrows are an important reflection of regional conditions.

Discussions of the relationship between the natural and man-made landscapes of the past feature prominently in archaeological literature. Many writers have recently concerned themselves with the location of monuments in relation to prominent landforms, be it hills, rocky outcrops, lakes and rivers, coastlines, unusual geological formations or particular types of rock (Tilley 1994; Vaquero Lastres 1999; Bradley 2000; Scarre 2002). We commented previously on the location of the long barrow cemeteries (and individual barrows) upon 'islands' – either natural elevations in boggy and marshy terrain or, as in the case of some cemeteries along the Seine and Yonne valleys, virtual islands defined by the seasonal flooding of the meandering river channels (*21*). The significance of such locations should not be underestimated. That water was essential to life goes without saying, but it seems also to have been important in death. The proximity of water may have symbolically distinguished between the worlds of the living and of the dead, playing an important role in the *rites de passage*. It was not necessary to surround the dead by water all the time. The symbolic division of space, either through periodic flooding or in the presence of marshy areas, would have ensured that the spirits of the dead were retained within their appropriate locales; a psychological barrier was sufficient for organising the space of the dead. In the case of the cemeteries on the banks of the Seine and Yonne, there may have been an additional element. The location of these sites low down by the river may have provided the very rare conditions for seeing these 'islands of the dead' from a bird's-eye view by those living and working along the edge of the plateaux above the rivers.

Water seems to have had a particular significance in the burial rituals of the Mesolithic – be it by the sea-coast, as at Téviec and Hoëdic, or in the proximity of deep water inlets in Scandinavia, as at Skateholm and Vedbæk and, indeed, on numerous Scandinavian shell-middens – and was one of the important elements in the hunter-gatherer cosmology. That it continued to play an important symbolic role within the TRB and the Cerny cultures is documented not only through the location of burial monuments but also in the tradition of votive offerings discussed in chapter 2. Such deposits, at the edges of lakes and in boggy environments, began in southern Scandinavia in the late Mesolithic. In the Neolithic they continued and included domesticated cattle, pottery, axes and occasionally human bodies; furthermore such votive places were never physically far from the burial monuments, be they long barrows or later megalithic tombs (Koch 1998). This is a clear legacy from the preceding hunter-gatherer tradition – a tradition not limited by geographical or cultural frontiers but one which retained and developed further an essential link with the past.

The predominant use of locally available raw materials is an important regional consideration. The earth and timber used in the construction of the long barrow cemeteries along the Seine and Yonne valleys reflects the lack of suitable large stones along the river plains, but it may also relate directly to the wooded conditions of some of the 'islands' within the meanders of the rivers. In contrast, along the North European Plain, the plentiful erratic boulders provided a suitable material for the subsequent retention of the earthen mounds. We have already noted that they were used in a 'raw' state; this was not because the builders were not capable of working the stone but rather because, even when employed as a kerb, such erratics may have resembled the formations naturally strewn across the landscape. The transformation of some of the Danish mounds from a timber to a stone version – most dramatically exemplified at Bygholm Nørremark – may, among other things, reflect the changing conditions of the cultivated landscape, with the trees being progressively cut to expose a landscape of rocks and boulders. Indeed, the past consideration of Breton mounds as more megalithic by virtue of the use of stone in the construction of chambers and cairns is another very obvious example of using, and perhaps imitating, what is natural locally.

The cultural location of the cemeteries also reveals pan-European characteristics, imbued with important symbolism. They are located within the core of the ancestral settlement zones, be it on the alluvial banks of the Yonne and Seine previously occupied by the late Danubian groups or in close proximity to contemporary late Danubian settlements, as seen in Kujavia. Future research will confirm whether Balloy is unique or typical in its intimate relationship between houses and barrows, but at least one reason for these regional differences seems to relate to regional chronologies.

In spite of the dearth of well-contexted radiocarbon dates, Kujavia nevertheless provides good evidence for at least partial contemporaneity of the Lengyel and the early TRB communities in this area; they were most certainly in contact with one another from the mid-fifth millennium BC, even if this involved only selected enclaves. Ryszard Grygiel, for example, has suggested that the inhabitants of house no. 56 from Brześć Kujawski were craftsmen who may well have come to the village from outside, from the realm of the TRB culture (Grygiel 1986, 261). They provided numerous services, manufacturing T-shaped antler axes, making jewellery from shell beads and cattle teeth and working hide, but lived on the periphery of the village, perhaps never fully integrated into the Lengyel community. It thus seems certain that at least some of the Lengyel villages continued to be inhabited at the time when TRB communities were establishing themselves across the North European Plain.

The relationship between the Villeneuve-Saint-Germain and Cerny cultures in northern France is more difficult to articulate. The radiocarbon dates are inconclusive, and so far there is no clear evidence for any prolonged overlap between the newly emerging Cerny groups and the late Danubians (Dubouloz 2003). Indeed, the evidence from Balloy would suggest that the Villeneuve-Saint-Germain settlements were by and large abandoned by the time the Cerny cemeteries were being established.

We should not be surprised that the long barrows in other areas, for example in north Germany and southern Scandinavia, developed a different distribution pattern. First of all, the Danubian settlement did not reach that far north, and the tradition of the Danubian village may have been known only from stories told about lands further to the south. This may have taken the form of reminiscences about rare visits to those distant regions or, indeed, been known simply from descriptions passed by word of mouth from those living at the southern edge of the Plain to those further north. There was no Danubian settlement so far north but the funerary code required that burials were placed in specific locations: the environmental conditions were easily satisfied as there was an abundance of water and marshy areas. The requirement of an ancestral place was translated, within the local context, into a single monument placed upon a recently abandoned settlement.

In spite of these differences, there is a strong cultural symbolism: on the one hand we see an intimate relationship with places of the ancestral past and, on the other, we note the ostentatious monumentality which imposes a new significance on the funerary sphere within the TRB and Cerny societies. Before we discuss these two important aspects we need to consider the status of the dead for whom the long barrows were raised.

STATUS OF THE DEAD

Even if we accept that the surviving long barrow cemeteries offer only a small sample of this form of burial, it is quite clear that only selected members of the community were provided with such an extraordinary placement; indeed, contemporary burials in flat cemeteries, within settlements and at other locations,confirm this beyond any doubt. The individuals buried within long barrows – either singly or at most a very few within one monument – were undoubtedly privileged members whom the community as a whole held in special regard. The inevitable question thus arises as to what were the criteria for the long barrow cemetery burial.

The tendency for certain individuals to be distinguished through burial ritual had, of course, commenced earlier. We have already reviewed arguments for an increasing social differentiation from the late *Linearbandkeramik* onwards, and the evidence certainly suggests that some individuals – adults as well as children – were treated in special ways. The evidence from late Mesolithic burials, while more ambiguous, nevertheless also suggests that some individuals were given different treatment, although whether this was on account of their standing within the local social hierarchy or because they held some other privileged position (for example accomplished hunters, community or spiritual leaders) is difficult to determine. Although the recognition of spiritual leaders – shamans – features quite prominently within the current archaeological interpretations of all periods (Price N. 2001; Strassburg 2000), not every anomalous burial need automatically represent a prehistoric shaman.

While our review of the human remains from the long barrow cemeteries highlighted the relative poverty of preservation, the evidence from the French sites has nevertheless confirmed that age and sex were not among the discriminating factors. Men and women as well as children of various ages were buried in the long barrow cemeteries and, as we have already seen, this is borne out in all other regions. Individual monuments within a cemetery, especially when they contain more than one grave, may reflect families or family groups. Interpretations are difficult to arrive at presently, but cemeteries with large series of burials may yield themselves to future DNA analyses, which would help to establish genetic relationships between the buried individuals and may thus shed light on the use of individual monuments as possible family mausolea.

Within the early TRB and Cerny cultures there is little outwith the funerary sphere to enlighten us on the status of such individuals or their families. The rather fleeting and insubstantial nature of the settlements does not provide us with any significant clues as to the way the communities may have organised themselves. There certainly are no indications of social differences in terms of abode or domestic tasks, although the latter must have been apportioned on a variety of levels; the presence of specialised craftsmen such as flint miners, potters or cattle breeders does not of itself imply social differentiation.

Some scholars have argued, for example, that the TRB and Cerny enclosures had come to represent places of central authority, indicative of the hierarchical structure of society. No TRB enclosures have so far been identified within areas of Kujavia or Western Pomerania, although it may be only a matter of time before they are discovered. The Scandinavian enclosures are closely associated with settled areas but they were not settlement sites, at least not at the time of their initial construction and use. A number of sites, such as Sarup (Andersen N.H. 1997, 101-28), became a focus for settlement only after they ceased to function as ceremonial sites. On present evidence most of these date from about the middle of the fourth millennium BC, thus postdating the beginning of the first monumental barrows.

The Cerny enclosures, while regarded by many scholars as settlements, equally reveal no traces of classic domestic debris. J.-P. Delor has proposed an interpretative model for the organisation of the Cerny settlement in the Yonne-Seine river valleys which is based on discrete territories. Each is identified by, among other things, a juxtaposition of enclosure and long barrow cemetery at its core, and the very large enclosures are said to replace the cemeteries at some later stage (*35*; Delor *et al.* 1997) The already discussed enclosure at Balloy, which appears to be contemporary with the use of the cemetery, does to a certain extent support such an interpretation. However, as we have already noted, there is little evidence to suggest that it functioned as a settlement and it could hardly be interpreted as a place of central authority.

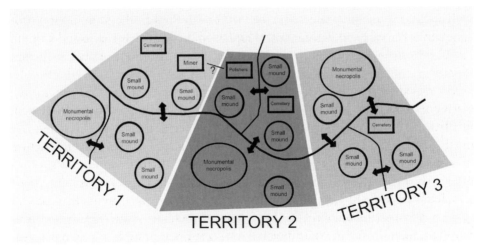

35 Territorial model of the Cerny culture in the Yonne-Seine valley based on the distribution of monumental cemeteries and enclosures. *Delor* et al. *1997*

Rather, in accordance with the interpretation of the Scandinavian enclosures, we should see such Cerny sites as ceremonial centres with activities involving deposition of selected items such as axes, pottery and animal remains – all highly structured and, on some occasions at least, relating to burial activities taking place only some distance away. Indeed, such sites may well represent the cumulative effect of numerous ceremonial acts – digging ditches, placing deposits, feasting – not all of which need be considered contemporary; they are the result of activities separate in time, engaging small, segmented communities in co-operative ventures.

Thus one needs to return to the burial evidence, that most ambivalent source of all. Chambon's recent analysis of the human remains from Passy and Balloy has highlighted an interesting aspect (Chambon 1997, 2003). The barrows within the central section of the Balloy cemetery have been identified as gender specific: adults buried in barrows II, V, VI and XVI were males; those in barrows I, XVIII, XV, XVII and IV were females (*36*). While the sex of the children contained within these monuments unfortunately could not be determined, not a single monument apparently contained adults of opposing sex. Chambon has argued that such arrangements were intentional acts of sexualisation with 'male' and 'female' monuments constructed as opposing pairs.

This pattern, fascinating though it is and potent with gender interpretations, unfortunately cannot at present be verified anywhere else. The pair of barrows at Gron contained exclusively male burials, and the interments at Passy do not follow this pattern either. Although Chambon has suggested pairings of barrows, they are based upon morphological features of the monuments and do not relate to the sex or age of the individuals concerned. Nor is such sexualisation of monuments observed anywhere else within the long barrow distribution.

In Kujavia, men and women have been found buried in the same barrow (for example barrows 2 and 8 at Sarnowo) and at Malice Kościelne men and women had also been buried side by side; other regions sadly do not provide sufficient evidence.

As noted previously, the grave goods, with rare exceptions, are scanty. Garments and jewellery accompanying the dead are expressions of personal identity and they vary in accordance with regional traditions: amber in the north, shell and hard stone predominantly in the west. The stereotypical nature of other deposits is seen in various combinations of bone and flint tools, occasional ceramics and food provisions. There are, however, certain types of goods which are worthy of particular consideration; we may thus single out the curious bone spatulas found in the French cemeteries, flint axes in southern Scandinavia and, in the wider north–west European context, the emphasis on hunting equipment within the funerary ritual of an agricultural community.

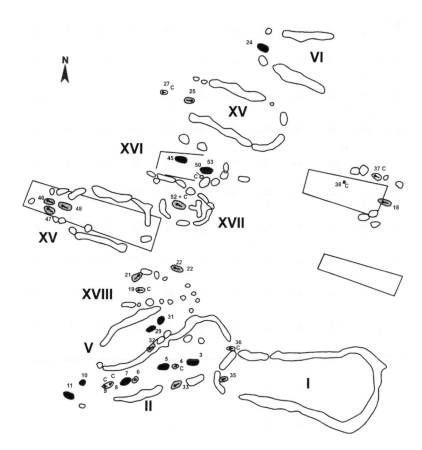

36 Central part of the cemetery from Balloy displaying 'male' and 'female' monuments. *Mordant 1997*

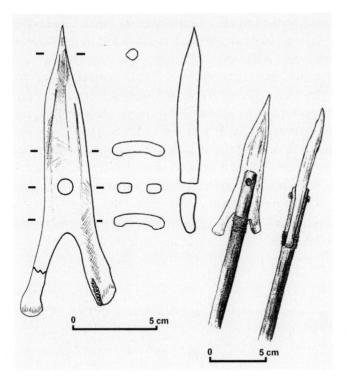

37 Reconstruction of the hafting of the so-called 'Eiffel Tower' bone spatula. *Sidéra 2000*

The curious bone spatulas from the Cerny context (the so-called *Tours Eiffel*) are objects, polished to a smooth flat finish, usually found near the head of the deceased. They have been the subject of intense speculation as to their role and function, and their strongly anthropomorphic symbolism has been emphasised by a number of French researchers (Carré 1993, Duhamel 1997). Isabelle Sidéra has recently argued that they can be interpreted equally plausibly as hafted bone spears rather than stylised female figurines (*37*; Sidéra 2000, 151). The bone spatulas have been found in association with males at Balloy, but the same cannot be confirmed for Passy. We may consider them for the time being as daggers or lances used by males for ceremonial purposes and regard them as markers of social distinction.

While flint axes are not significantly represented within the core area of the long barrow cemeteries, they seem to play a role on the periphery of the barrow distribution. The importance of flint axes within the Nordic tradition has already been discussed (chapter 2) and their association with burial can be traced back to the Ertebølle culture, with the exotic Danubian *Schuhleistenkeile* providing the most poignant examples. The high symbolic prestige of the flint axes was directly related to their economic potential – a commodity which sustained more than any other the inter-regional exchange power of the Scandinavian TRB communities. The axe was an important link between the economic and ceremonial spheres: its placement in the graves, apart from high-lighting the prestige of the individual, connected the dead with the wider world of the spirits appeased through the votive offerings in marshes and other watery locations. Thus it linked public and private areas within the new set of commitments and ideologies.

In Armorica and Normandy, axes often made of exotic materials were also employed in votive deposits, either placed under the standing menhirs, or in association with burial monuments (for example the seven jade axes found in the early nineteenth century at Sarceaux; Chancerel and Desloges 1998). The chronology of the erection of standing stones is notoriously difficult, but recent reassessment of this phenomenon from the area of central Alentejo, Portugal, has tentatively suggested that these may relate to the transition from the late Mesolithic to the Neolithic. Here, however, we are faced with a diametrically opposite situation whereby the water-rich estuaries are being abandoned for the arid and stony interior (Calado 2002).

Hunting symbolism

The symbolism evoked through the placement of hunting equipment within the long barrow graves is equally important for our understanding of the social and ideological changes taking place around the middle of the fifth millennium BC, when the hunting of wild animals as an economic activity is in slow but progressive decline. We have already discussed the various aspects of the agricultural nature of the TRB and Cerny cultures and explored the increasing role of cereals and domesticated animals within the economy. However, when we consider the burial ritual, we could be excused for believing that we are dealing with a hunting community. Such, indeed, was the mistake made by Ewald Schuldt, who excavated several TRB flat cemeteries in the central lake belt in Mecklenburg, of which Ostorf is the best known example (Schuldt 1961). These were not 'monumental' cemeteries but the dead, placed in simple flat graves, were accompanied by generous grave goods: elaborate jewellery made from bones and teeth of wild animals, and hunting equipment in the form of quiverfuls of arrows. On the basis of this – what Schuldt referred to as 'hunters' trophies' – these cemeteries were interpreted as representative of economically and culturally backward groups who, while aware of farmers, were themselves essentially hunter-gatherers.

The analysis of grave goods from the long barrow cemeteries presents a similar picture. While the iconography of the rare ceramic vessels found within the French long barrow cemeteries evokes bovine symbolism (stylised cattle bucrania), hunting is evoked in the context of both sexes (as a quiver with twelve arrows accompanying the young female in grave 4.1 at Passy confirms) according to strict codes, which involve deposition of bone points and arrows – sometimes as mere tokens, at other times as bundles of up to 22 in a quiver. This is further emphasised in 'hunters' trophies': antler objects, necklaces of wild animal teeth or massive boars' tusks (indicative of huge and dangerous animals and known from Kujavia as well as from the south Paris Basin) fashioned into bracelets or head ornaments, all suggesting a 'victory' status. Sidéra has argued that hunting equipment may have been a broader social signifier, reflecting not merely prowess in such a privileged and specialised activity as hunting but equally standing for accomplishments in leadership, in competition and in warfare. In terms of placement in the graves, these are predominantly, but not exclusively, male attributes and their symbolism may be related equally strongly to the autochthonous nature of the TRB and Cerny communities, whose ancestry was deeply rooted in the local hunting-gathering background. Paradoxically, the 'hunt' seems to have been appropriated as a new social signifier and a new code for the farmer.

Thus while the grave goods, as various social signifiers, suggest to us that the individuals buried within the long barrow cemeteries may have held important social positions within their respective communities, we are nonetheless in a situation no better than when we tried to interpret the possible levels of social differences within the late Mesolithic and Danubian communities. We have noted earlier the characteristics of the Danubian communities which, according to Jeunesse, express a society in the process of increasing social differentiation, with the emergence of a strong hereditary element. Equally, we have observed comments by Bogucki, on the nature of transegalitarian societies where fierce competition and alliances can lead to substantial differences between groups and individuals, without such differences necessarily becoming hereditary.

There have been various attempts at definition of the criteria which permit us to identify past social hierarchies. Within the continental context of the post-Danubian world, scholars who subscribe to evolutionary social models have suggested a number of archaeological indicators which could be used to define complex past societies. Prominent among them are: structured settlements, sexual task differentiation, industrial activities such as flint mining, hierarchical social organisation which integrates children, presence of specific ceremonial sites – including monumental funerary architecture – and votive deposits (Lichardus 1991). However, all but one – funerary monumentality – can be associated with the lifestyles of the late hunter-gatherers and Danubian communities. It is therefore to that monumentality and its source that we must now turn.

ANCESTRAL PASTS AND FUTURES: FROM VILLAGES TO MONUMENTAL CEMETERIES

There are a sufficient number of Kujavian long barrow cemeteries displaying the fan-like arrangement of mounds – frequently in groups of three – to confirm that this was not a haphazard pattern, but rather a layout which followed a preconceived model. The spatial arrangements of the houses from the Brześć Kujawski settlement, which is typical of many other Lengyel sites in Kujavia, and the long barrows from Sarnowo (*22*) have been compared by myself as well as others (Midgley 1985, 213-15; Bradley 1998b, 46-8). The layout of the trapezoidal houses suggests that contemporary households are represented by groups of three houses (*23*; for example cluster B with houses 11, 13 and 15; cluster D with houses 8, 12 and 20 or cluster A with houses 2, 4 and 6). When we compare this arrangement with that of the cemetery at Sarnowo – and, indeed, other Kujavian cemeteries such as Leśniczówka, Obałki, Wietrzychowice or Zberzyn (Midgley 1985, Fig. 23) – the similarity is very striking indeed, and the inescapable conclusion has to be that the Kujavian cemeteries were modelled on the Lengyel settlements. Indeed, in the concluding part of my doctoral thesis I wrote:

> Short of the discovery of a long barrow constructed upon a disused long house, the situation evidenced in Kujavia offers the strongest arguments yet for accepting the derivation of the northern long barrow from the long house (Midgley 1985, 215).

Naturally, I could hardly have known that in that same year the Balloy cemetery would be discovered from the air.

The structural principles of this site are not in doubt: as discussed earlier, the Balloy cemetery was placed upon an abandoned Villeneuve-Saint-Germain settlement with at least five of the Cerny long mounds being placed directly upon the older long houses, with the latter influencing the orientation and, at least in part, the morphology of the burial mounds. Moreover, we have also suggested that those partaking in funerary activities not only were aware of the ancientness of this place but could hardly avoid knowing that they were digging the graves within the foundations of old houses.

The cemetery at Passy offers a much more complex layout, with the long period of use of this site, as well as partial destruction prior to the excavation, making analysis more difficult. Nevertheless, as Chambon (2003) recently suggested, the barrows at Passy were not laid out haphazardly but the construction followed an internal logic. The individual barrows differ in size and shape ,but one can identify complementary groups of three or two monuments which relate to one another through their spatial positioning, orientation and architectural details of eastern façades: an entrance and/or placement of timber posts – the latter plausible totemic group markers – are present in one monument of each group.

It would be unreasonable to expect all long barrow cemeteries to follow these particular principles, as they were clearly constructed to reflect the specific needs of individual communities. Indeed, in areas where barrow construction commenced later – for example in southern Scandinavia – individual monuments rather than cemeteries seemed appropriate to local circumstances. Nevertheless, at the two extremes of the long barrow cemetery distribution – in the south Paris Basin and in Kujavia – we observe the same general principles: the villages of the late Danubian groups dramatically influence the form and layout of the monumental cemeteries, a pattern which is even more intriguing by virtue of the vast geographical distance separating the two regions.

The idea of a house of the living serving as a prototype for a house of the dead has a long ancestry. It goes back at least to the mid-nineteenth century, with the Swede Sven Nilsson speculating on the similarities between the ground plans of Eskimo houses and Swedish passage graves (Nilsson 1868). Oscar Montelius followed this idea in his own interpretation of megalithic tombs (Montelius 1905), and even Sprockhoff (1938) noted that German long barrows may have resembled long houses in their external appearance. However, the most dramatic impact came from Gordon Childe's suggestion that the north European long barrows approximated to the habitations discovered at the late Danubian settlement at Brześć Kujawski (Childe 1949, 135). Many British scholars investigating long barrows in the 1960s and 1970s expressed general confidence in this comparison; more recently Hodder (1984) and Bradley (1998b, 2002) have explored the concept of the Danubian long house as a model for the long barrow in some detail, and the French Neolithic specialists are now also in sympathy with this idea (Duhamel 1997; Mordant 1997, 1998).

The Danubian long houses have, of course, fascinated archaeologists since their first appearance in the archaeological record at the beginning of the twentieth century. Initially misinterpreted as the remains of barns (after Buttler and Haberey's excavations at Köln-Lindenthal; 1936), their reassessment by Oscar Paret in the late 1940s (Paret 1948) – subsequently confirmed by numerous studies – provided us with the first substantial, man-made structures in central and north-west Europe.

We need not concern ourselves with precise details of the construction of long houses, since this subject has been covered in numerous monographs (von Brandt 1988; Coudart 1998; Pavlu° 2000). It is, however, worthwhile to comment on a number of general themes. Within the variation offered by the ground plans, we may nevertheless note a consistent design, with three rows of roof-bearing posts creating a four-aisled building, with up to three linearly arranged segments, and with each of the segments demarcated to the outside by the lateral pits. This design is in itself suggestive of a very strong symbolism in the use and function of such structures over their vast distribution area from Slovakia in the east to the Paris Basin in the west.

Indeed, Bradley has recently stated that 'the houses themselves are almost too big, too monumental, with the result that they are too difficult to interpret entirely in terms of the routines of daily life' (Bradley 2002, 20) and that their significance extended beyond everyday considerations. His comment that the houses show little evidence of repair, but that they were frequently abandoned while structurally still sound, is particularly important. A number of years ago I made the point that our image of the early Danubian village needs dramatic reinterpretation (Midgley 1997a). One of the fascinating features of the *Linearbandkeramik* villages is the fact that, with rare exceptions, there is virtually no overlap between the house plans. New houses were built on a new plot of land and not on the spot where the earlier houses stood; in effect, the LBK villages were spreading horizontally over considerable areas of the landscape. Only within some of the very late Danubian villages, such as those of the Lengyel Brześć Kujawski group, is there any overlap; here houses seem to have been rebuilt more or less exactly on the same spot (Grygiel 1986).

Different explanations have been suggested for the pattern of the *Linearbandkeramik* villages, but none was entirely satisfactory. Why structurally sound buildings should have been abandoned or, at least, why generally little effort was made to maintain them after a certain period, is difficult to explain. The building of such a house – selecting the right trees, cutting them down, transporting and preparing the timbers for posts and planks etc. – must have involved considerable effort, not just on the part of a few family members but, undoubtedly, by the larger community. The concept of labour involved in the building of an LBK house, however, need not correspond to our own and the amount of work may have been insignificant to the builders; constructing a new house by engaging many individuals may well have continued to be one of the different ways of creating a sense of communal belonging.

While there is precious little evidence for the superstructure and the floor level of the houses, in recent years more examples of houses associated with burials have come to light – not just burials in the external lateral pits but, on rare occasions, within the confines of the foundations. We have noted such examples earlier (chapter 3) and it is not unreasonable to suggest that the death of a particular inhabitant may have made it necessary to abandon the house altogether. Indeed such a location, where a long house originally stood, may have been considered unsuitable for a new habitation because an abandoned or derelict house – with or without the dead intimately associated with it – was regarded as sacred, representing a powerful ancestral space. Thus, within the LBK one did not live on top of the ancestors (as was the case on some Mesolithic sites and clearly practised in the south-east of Europe) but built a new house at some distance away. If such an idea is acceptable, then our interpretation of the appearance of the LBK settlement has developed along lines very different from what such a village may really have looked like. Abandoned or unoccupied houses would have stood side by side with those that were in use. The former in due course would have become dilapidated ruins (*colour plate 21*); overgrown and covered with blown earth, they may have appeared as artificial mounds – models for future burial mounds.*

---

*Indeed, the ruins of a Danubian house reconstructed by Claude Constantin in 1977, and burnt by local youths a few years later, at Cuiry-lès-Chaudardes provide an example of what an abandoned LBK house may have looked like. The remaining timber uprights of the external walls may provide prototypes for the timber uprights erected in some of the French long barrow ditches.

Until recently arguments about the visibility of ruined Danubian houses have been largely academic, relying mainly upon the lack of overlap between buildings of different phases on LBK settlements. That this is more than just a theoretical assumption has now been demonstrated quite dramatically in northern Poland. Rescue excavations along a projected gas pipeline from the Yamal peninsula in north-west Siberia to western Europe identified over 700 sites of archaeological interest, among them the spectacular discoveries of the early and late Danubian settlements at Bożejewice, near Strzelno in Kujavia (Czerniak 1998). Here foundations of a classic rectangular LBK house, 43m long and 6.5 to 7.3m wide, were discovered. Within them, aligned precisely along the main axis and effectively contained within the original foundations, was a smaller, trapezoidal late Danubian house (*colour plate 22*). The LBK house is dated to the later sixth millennium BC while the trapezoidal house, typical of the Lengyel Brześć Kujawski group in the region, can hardly be dated much before the mid–fifth millennium BC. Thus several centuries separate the two structures, and yet such precise positioning of one house within the other can hardly be accidental.

The preliminary excavation report is brief and we do not know how this particular house remained visible for so many centuries: were the timber uprights, dried up in the wind, still protruding from the foundations? Was there an earthen mound which had accumulated within the collapsed walls? What is clear is that this LBK house was marked on the ground in such a way as to permit a precise superimposition of a later building.

We may further ask whether such a positioning was due simply to the visibility of the old foundations or whether there was any symbolic significance in locating, several centuries later, another house in this precise spot. We are not considering here the 'ancestral' quality that initially prevented the construction of new houses upon older buildings. Quite to the contrary, the fortuitous example of the Bożejewice house demonstrates the secondary, mythical value of the old settlement. Indeed, we could suggest that, in this case, the old ruined house was made 'alive' once again – was it perhaps the first building in the construction of a new Lengyel settlement? Was it important to begin a new village by some reference to a mythical settlement from the past?

It is precisely within this symbolic concept of relating the past to the future that we need to consider the relationship between the Danubian villages and long barrow cemeteries. Previously, we have concentrated upon the morphological similarities between the long houses and long mounds, comparing the size, proportions and other individual features. The recognition that a collapsed long house may have looked like an artificial mound provides us with an intellectual as well as a real model for the man-made long barrow (*38*).

In my interpretation of the North European long barrow cemeteries, I argued that the barrows of the TRB culture imitate the layout and design of the long-house villages of the local Lengyel tradition (Midgley 1985, 215).

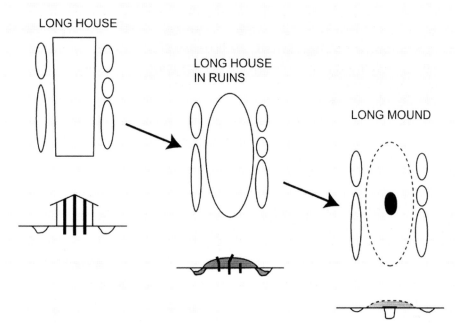

38 Theoretical model for the transformation of a house of the living into a house of the dead

However, at that time, I did not develop this argument any further and it was not until the plans of the monumental cemeteries from the Seine and Yonne river valleys were published – especially the dramatic evidence from Balloy – that I was struck by the extraordinary interpretational potential of such arrangements.

An abandoned Danubian village – in the same manner as an abandoned medieval village so easily recognised by us today – stood in magnificent ruin, clearly visible in the landscape. It was not only a reminder but also a powerful symbol of permanence and ancestry in the form of a village of solidly built houses; the tradition of a village in which the ancestors – in the guise of their dilapidated homes – were constantly side by side with the living must have been still fresh in the memory of the communities. While the vernacular tradition of those times is sadly not available to us today, we would be wrong to assume that there was not an entire store of tales, songs, superstitions and myths associated with such abandoned villages. They may have been visited on special occasions – or perhaps, to the contrary, avoided as frightening and dangerous places – but they were permanently imprinted on the landscape.

While there are indeed similarities between the long barrows and long houses, a house was merely a component of a village, one of many elements that symbolise families coming together to form a community. Thus the significance of the long barrow cemeteries does not lie in monumentalising the long house, but in monumentalising the entire ancestral village. It was the entire community and not the individual household that was important, and it is that concept of community that became symbolised through the long barrow cemeteries. By the time that the earthen long barrows were being constructed in north-west Europe, the original LBK villages were a distant memory – symbols of the mythical arrival of the first farmers onto new lands. It was this symbol that was transferred from a domestic to a funerary sphere and which became the most powerful and enduring contribution of the Danubian farmers to the new world which they helped to forge.

Finally, we need to ask why this symbolism – of a mythical village of ancestors – should have assumed such monumental quality. The idea of monumentality, especially in the context of the north-west European megalithic tradition, has been addressed many times in archaeological literature. Monumentality has been variously seen as a claim to control of a territory and its natural resources, a signifier of social hierarchies or an ideological statement of a ruling elite (Casal 1997; Le Roux 1992; Renfrew 1973, 1976; Shanks and Tilley 1982; Sherratt 1990, 1995; Trigger 1990).

The term 'monument' derives from the Latin *monere* ('to remind', 'to warn'); the Oxford English Dictionary defines monument as 'a statue, building, or other structure erected to commemorate a notable person or event', as 'an enduring and memorable example or reminder' and monumental is defined as 'great in importance, extent, or size'. In this sense archaeologists have commonly used these terms to denote structures whose '...scale and elaboration exceed the requirements of any practical function' they are designed to perform (Trigger 1990, 119).

Against such a commonsense definition there is little doubt that the long barrow cemeteries fulfil the criteria of monumentality, reflecting each and every one of the concepts behind this definition. As individual structures, the long mounds were large, indeed much larger than was necessary to cover the graves within them, with some reaching gigantic proportions. Even if they were not particularly high (up to 1m in height and often less) they were designed to be lasting and impressive, and in many cases the builders employed simple perspective to enhance that image further. Grouped in cemeteries, they created an even more dramatic effect – constructed to be seen and to impress those who saw them (*colour plate 23*).

We have already seen that within the late Mesolithic and the Danubian burial traditions, certain selected dead had been afforded specific and elaborate burial treatment. Specific locations could be selected, significant acts performed prior to or during the burial, and deliberately chosen items deposited with the dead to distinguish them from others; some may have assumed the important status of ancestors. However, these differentiations were part of the actual burial ceremonies and, while they may have been known to and subsequently remembered by the participants, they were largely invisible afterwards.

The TRB and Cerny communities altered this dramatically. That ancestral values were important to these new farming communities is clearly demonstrated in the subtle merging of the late Mesolithic and Danubian ideals: that of individual social prestige and that of the collective identity. That an emphasis on such attributes should have been important in the context of burial practices is perhaps not surprising. The innovation lies in the vision which moved these values outside the realm of the past.

By intentionally incorporating architecture into the funerary sphere they created, within a complex ceremonial landscape, resting places for their important dead. Not only was the long barrow cemetery monumental in size but, more importantly, from its very beginning it was monumental in conception. The families who, in their various capacities, had contributed to the success and well-being of a community were to be buried with ostentatious ritual and, moreover, their privileged position was to be visible at all times. By linking elements of the past with those of the future, these communities provided an enduring home for their most revered dead.

REFERENCES

Albrethsen, S.E. and Brinch Petersen, E. 1977 Excavation of a Mesolithic cemetery at Vedbæk, Denmark, *Acta Archaeologica* 47, 1-28

Ammerman, A.J. 1989 On the Neolithic transition in Europe: a comment on Zvelebil and Zvelebil (1988), *Antiquity* 63, 162-65

Ammerman, A.J. and Cavalli-Sforza, L.L. 1973 A population model for the diffusion of early farming in Europe. In: C. Renfrew (ed) *The explanation of culture change: models in prehistory*, Duckworth, London, 343-57

Andersen, N.H. 1997 *Sarup Vol. 1: The Sarup Enclosures,* Jutland Archaeological Society Publications XXXIII: 1, Moesgaard

Andersen, S.H. 1993 Bjørnsholm. A stratified køkkenmødding on the Central Limfjord, North Jutland, *Journal of Danish Archaeology* 10, 59-96

Andersen, S.H. 1998 The Stone Age Coast – Visborg, *Marine Archaeology Newsletter from Roskilde Denmark* 11, 12-13

Andersen, S.H. 2000a Visborg (News and notes), *Marine Archaeology Newsletter from Roskilde Denmark* 13, 36-37

Andersen, S.H. 2000b 'Køkkenmøddinger' (shell-middens) in Denmark: a Survey, *Proceedings of the Prehistoric Society* 66, 361-84

Andersen, S.H. and Johansen, E. 1987 Ertebølle revisited. *Journal of Danish Archaeology* 5, 31-61

Andersen, S.H. and Johansen, E. 1992 An Early Neolithic Grave at Bjørnsholm, North Jutland, *Journal of Danish Archaeology* 9 (1990), 38-58

Andersen, S.Th. 1988 Pollen Spectra from the Double Passage-Grave, Klekkendehøj, on Møn. Evidence of Swidden Cultivation in the Neolithic of Denmark, *Journal of Danish Archaeology* 7, 77-92

Andersen, S.Th. 1990 Pollen Spectra from two Early Neolithic Lugged Jars in the Long Barrow of Bjørnsholm, Denmark, *Journal of Danish Archaeology* 9, 59-63

Andersen, S.Th. 1995 Pollen analytical investigations of barrows from the Funnel Beaker and Single Grave cultures in the Vroue area, West Jutland, Denmark, *Journal of Danish Archaeology* 12, 107-132

Arts, N. and Hoogland, M. 1987 A Mesolithic settlement area with a human cremation grave at Oirschot V, municipality of Best, the Netherlands, *Helinium* 27, 172-89

Augereau, A. 1993 *Évolution de l'industrie du silex du Ve et IVe millénaire avant J.-C. dans le sud-est du Bassin Parisien. Organisation techno-économique de Villeneuve-Saint-Germain au groupe de Noyen: l'apport des études lithiques*, Thèse présentée en Préhistoire-Ethnologie-Anthropologie, Université de Paris I Panthéon, Sorbonne

Augereau, A. and Mordant, D. 1993 L'Enceinte Néolithique Cerny des Réaudins à Balloy (Seine-et-Marne), *Mémoires du Groupement Archéologique de Seine-et-Marne* 1, 97-109

Augereau, A., Gouge, P., Mordant, D. and Tresset, A. 1992 Une vaste opération de sauvetage archéologique en cours à Balloy (Seine-et-Marne), *Bulletin du Groupement Archéologique de Seine-et-Marne* 28-31 (1987-1990), 75-97

Bagge, A. and Kaelas, L. 1950/1952 *Die Funde aus Dolmen und Ganggräbern in Schonen, Schweden*, Wahlström and Wildstrand, Stockholm, (vol. I 1950; vol. II 1952)

Bailloud, G. 1964 *Le Néolithique dans le Bassin parisien*. Gallia Préhistoire, 2e Supplément, CNRS, Paris

Bakker J.A. 1976 On the Possibility of Reconstructing Roads from the TRB period, *Berichten van de Rijksdienst voor het Oudheidkundig Bodemonderzoek*, 26, 63-91

Bakker, J.A. 1992 *The Dutch Hunebeden. Megalithic Tombs of the Funnel Beaker Culture*. International Monographs in Prehistory, Archaeological Series 2, Ann Arbor, Michigan

Bakker, J.A., Kruk, J., Lanting, A.E. and Milisauskas, S. 1999 The earliest evidence of wheeled vehicles in Europe and the Near East, *Antiquity* 73, 778-90

Balcer, B. 1975 *Krzemień Świeciechówski w Kulturze Pucharów Lejkowatych. Eksploatacja, obróbka i rozprzestrzenienie*, Ossolineum, Wrocław

Bargieł, B., Florek, M. and Libera, J. 1998 Drugi sezon badań cmentarzyska neolity-cznego w Malicach Kościelnych stan. 1, woj. Tarnobrzeskie, *Archeologia Polski Środkowowschodniej* 3, 44-55

Bazzanella, M. 1997 Les vases à ouverture carrée en Europe occidentale. In: C. Constantin, D. Mordant and D. Simonin (eds) *La Culture de Cerny. Nouvelle économie, nouvelle société au Néolithique*, Actes du Colloque International de Nemours 1994, Mémoires du Musée de Préhistoire d'Île-de-France 6, 557-74

Bednarczyk, J., Czerniak, L. and Kośko, A. 1980 Z badań nad zespołem osadniczym ludności z kręgu kultur ceramiki wstęgowej w Kruszy Zamkowej, stan. 3. woj. Bydgoszcz, *Sprawozdania Archeologiczne* 32, 55-83

Behrends, R.-H. 1997 La nécropole rubanée de Schwetzingen (Kr. Rhin-Neckar, Bade-Wurtemberg). In: C. Jeunesse (ed) *Le Néolithique danubien et ses marges entre Rhin et Seine*, XXIIe colloque interrégional sur le Néolithique Strasbourg 27-29 octobre 1995, Cahiers de l'Association pour la Promotion de la Recherche Archéologique en Alsace, Supplément 3, Strasbourg, 17–29

Beltz, R. 1910 *Die vorgeschichtlichen Altertümer des Großherzogtums Mecklenburg*, Schwerin

Bentley, A.R., Chikhi, L. and Price, T.D. 2003 The Neolithic transition in Europe: comparing broad scale genetic and local scale isotopic evidence, *Antiquity* 77, 63–66

Bernardini, O., Delneuf, M., Fonton, M., Peyre, E. and Sidéra, I. 1992 La sépulture «Grossgartach» de la Sablonnière à Passy (Yonne): aspects archéologiques. *Actes du 11ᵉ colloque interrégional sur le Néolithique*, Mulhouse, 5-6-7 octobre 1984, Association INTERNEO, Saint-Germain-en-Laye, 119–30

Billard, C., Arbogast, R.-M., Valentin, F. 2001 La sépulture mésolithique des Varennes à Val-de-Reuil (Eure), *Bulletin de la Société Préhistorique Française* 98 (1), 25–52

Binford, L.R. 1971 Mortuary practices: Their study and their potential. In: J.A. Brown (ed) *Approaches to the social dimensions of mortuary practices,* Society for American Archaeology, Memoirs 25, 6–29

Bødker Enghoff, I. 1995 Fishing in Denmark during the Mesolithic Period. In: A. Fischer (ed) *Man and Sea in the Mesolithic: Coastal settlement above and below present sea level.* Proceedings of the International Symposium, Kalundborg, Denmark 1993, Oxbow Books (Oxbow Monograph 53), Oxford, 67–74

Bogucki, P. 1993 Animal traction and household economies in Neolithic Europe, *Antiquity* 67, 492–503

Bogucki, P. 2000 How agriculture came to north-central Europe. In: T.D. Price (ed) *Europe's First Farmers*, Cambridge University Press, Cambridge, 197–218

Bogucki, P. 2003 Transegalitarian Societies in Mid-Neolithic Europe, 5000-3000 BC, paper presented at 'Heterarchy and Hierarchy in European Prehistory' a symposium in honor of Bernard Wailes on the occasion of his retirement at the University Museum, University of Pennsylvania, April 5, 2000 (manuscript)

Boujot, C. and Cassen, S. 1992 Le développement des premières architectures funéraires monumentales en France occidentale. In: *Paysans et bâtisseurs: l'émergence du Néolithique atlantique et les origines du mégalithisme*. Actes du 17ᵉ Colloque interrégional sur le Néolithique, Vannes, 29-31 octobre 1990. Revue Archéologique de l'Ouest, Supplément 5, 1992, 195–211

Boujot, C. and Cassen, S. 1993 A pattern of evolution for the Neolithic funerary structures of the west of France, *Antiquity* 67, 477–91

Bradley, R. 1998a *The Passage of Arms. An archaeological analysis of prehistoric hoard and votive deposits*, Oxbow Books, Oxford, (Second edition)

Bradley, R. 1998b *The Significance of Monuments. On the shaping of human experience in Neolithic and Bronze Age Europe*, Routledge, London

Bradley R. 2000 *An Archaeology of Natural Places*, Routledge, London

Bradley, R. 2001 Orientations and origins: a symbolic dimension to the long house in Neolithic Europe, *Antiquity* 75, 50–56

Bradley, R. 2002 *The Past in Prehistoric Societies*, Routledge, London

Brandt, D. von 1988 Häuser. In: U. Boelicke, D. von Brandt, J. Lüning, P. Stehli, A. Zimmermann, Der bandkeramische Siedlungsplatz Langweiler 8, Gemeinde Aldenhoven, Kreis Düren, *Rheinische Augrabungen* 28, Rheinland-Verlag, Köln, 36-289

Brandt, K. 1967 *Neolithische Siedlungsplätze im Stadtgebiet von Bochum*. Quellenschriften zur westdeutschen Vor- und Frühgeschichte 8, Bonn

Brinch Petersen, E. and Meiklejohn, C. 2003 Three Cremations and a Funeral: Aspects of Burial Practice in Mesolithic Vedbæk. In: L. Larsson, H. Kindgren, K. Knutsson, D. Loeffler and A. Åkerlund (eds) *Mesolithic on the Move. Papers Presented at the Sixth International Conference on the Mesolithic in Europe, Stockholm 2000, Oxbow Books, Oxford, 485-93*

Burchard, B. 1998 Badania grobowców typu megalitycznego w Zagaju Stradowskim w południowej Polsce, Sprawozdania Archeologiczne 50, 149-56

Buttler, W. and Haberey, W. 1936 Die bandkeramische Ansiedlung bei Köln-Lindenthal, Walter-Gruyter, Berlin-Leipzig

Calado, M. 2002 Standing stones and natural outcrops. The role of ritual monuments in the Neolithic transition of the Central Alentejo. In: C. Scarre (ed) *Monuments and Landscape in Atlantic Europe. Perception and Society during the Neolithic and Early Bronze Age*, Routledge, London, 17-35

Carr, C. 1995 Mortuary Practices: Their Social, Philosophical-Religious, Circumstantial, and Physical Determinants, *Journal of Archaeological Method and Theory* 2:2, 105-200

Carré, H. 1993 Spatules, statuettes, état de la pensée et culte au Néolithique. In: *Le Néolithique du nord-est de la France et des régions limitrophes, Actes du XIIIe colloque interrégional sur le Néolithique, Metz, 10, 11 et 12 octobre 1986*, Éditions de la Maison des Sciences et de l'Homme, Paris, 145-50

Casal, A.A.R. (ed) 1997 *O Neolítico Atlántico e as Orixes do Megalitismo*, Acta do Coloquio Internacional (Santiago de Compostela, 1-6 de abril de 1996), Universidade de Santiago de Compostela

Cassen, S., Boujot, C. and Vaquero, J. 2000 *Éléments d'architecture. Exploration d'un tertre funéraire à Lannec er Gadouer (Erdeven, Morbihan). Construction et reconstructions dans le Néolithique morbihannais. Propositions pour une lecture symbolique*, Association des Publications Chauvinoises, Chauvigny

Cauwe, N. 2001 *L'Héritage des chasseurs-cueilleurs dans le Nord-Ouest de l'Europe (10,000 – 3,000 avant notre ère)*, Éditions Errance, Paris

Chambon, P. 1997 La nécropole de Balloy «Les Réaudins»: approche archéo-anthropologique. In: C. Constantin, D. Mordant and D. Simonin (eds) *La culture de Cerny. Nouvelle économie, nouvelle société au Néolithique*. Actes du Colloque international de Nemours, 9-10-11 mai 1994, Mémoires du Musée de Préhistoire d'Île-de-France 6, 489-98

Chambon, P. 2003 Revoir Passy à la lumière de Balloy : les nécropoles monumentales Cerny du bassin Seine-Yonne, *Bulletin de la Société Préhistorique Française* 100 (3), 505-15

Chambon, P. and Lanchon, Y. 2001 Les structures sépulcrales de la nécropole de la Porte aux Bergers (Vignely, Seine et Marne), Pratiques funéraires du Néolithique ancien et moyen (en France et dans les régions limitrophes, entre 5000 et 3500 environ av. J.-C.), Musée des Antiquités Nationales, Saint-Germain-en-Laye 15, 16, 17 juin 2001, Résumés des communications, 25-6

Chancerel, A. and Desloges, J. 1998 Les sépultures pré-mégalithiques de Basse-Normandie. In: J. Guilaine (ed) *Sépultures d'Occident et genèses des mégalithismes (9000-3500 avant notre ère), Séminaire du Collège de France*, Éditions Errance, Paris, 91-106

Chancerel, A., Desloges, J., Dron, J.-L. and San Juan, G. 1992 Le début du Néolithique en Basse-Normandie. In: *Paysans et bâtisseurs: l'émergence du Néolithique atlantique et les origines du mégalithisme*. Actes du 17ᵉ colloque interrégional sur le Néolithique, Vannes, 29-31 octobre 1990. Revue Archéologique de l'Ouest, Supplément 5, 1992, 153-73

Chapman, R., Kinnes, I. and Randsborg, K. (eds) 1981 *The archaeology of death*, New Directions in Archaeology, Cambridge University Press, Cambridge

Childe, V.G. 1929 *The Danube in Prehistory*, Clarendon Press, Oxford

Childe, V.G. 1949 The Origins of Neolithic culture in northern Europe, *Antiquity* 32, 129-35

Constantin, C. 1985 *Fin du Rubané, céramique du Limbourg et post-Rubané. Le Néolithique le plus ancien en Bassin Parisien et en Hainaut*, BAR Inter. Series 273, Oxford

Constantin, C. 1997 Du groupe de Villeneuve-Saint-Germain à la Culture de Cerny. La céramique. In: C. Constantin, D. Mordant and D. Simonin (eds) *La Culture de Cerny. Nouvelle économie, nouvelle société au Néolithique*, Actes du Colloque International de Nemours 1994, Mémoires du Musée de Préhistoire d'Île-de-France 6, 65-71

Coudart, A. 1998 *Architecture et société néolithique. L'unité et la variance de la maison danubienne*, Éditions de la Maison des Sciences de l'Homme, Paris

Courtaud, P., Duday, H., Martin, H. and Robin, K. 1999 La nécropole mésolithique de La Vergne (Charente-Maritime, France). In: A. Thévenin (ed) *L'Europe des derniers chasseurs. Epipaléolithique et Mésolithique*, Actes du 5ᵉ Colloque International UISPP, Commission XII, Grenoble, 18-23 septembre 1995, Éditions du CTHS, Paris, 287-92

Czerniak, L. 1994 *Wczesny i Środkowy Okres Neolitu na Kujawach 5400–3650 p.n.e.*, Polska Akademia Nauk, Instytut Archeologii i Etnologii, Poznań

Czerniak, L. 1998 The First Farmers. In: *Pipeline of Archaeological Treasures*, (EuRoPol GAZ s.a.), Poznańskie Towarzystwo Prehistoryczne, Poznań, 23-36

Czerniak, L. 2002 Settlements of the Brześć Kujawski type on the Polish Lowlands, *Archeologické rozhledy* 54 (1), 9-22 (Festschrift for Marie Zápotocká)

Delor, J.-P., Genreau, F., Heurtaux, A., Jacob, J.-P., Leredde, H., Nouvel, P. and Pellet, C. 1997 L'implantation des nécropoles monumentales au sud du Bassin Parisien. In: C. Constantin, D. Mordant and D. Simonin (eds) *La Culture de Cerny. Nouvelle économie, nouvelle société au Néolithique*, Actes du Colloque International de

Nemours 9-10-11 mai 1994, Mémoires du Musée de Préhistoire d'Île-de-France 6, 381-95

Desloges, J.-P. 1986 Fouilles de mines à silex sur le site néolithique de Bretteville-le-Rabet (Calvados). In: *Actes du Xe colloque interrégional sur le Néolithique, Caen 30 septembre–2 octobre 1983*, Revue Archéologique de l'Ouest, Supplément 1, 73-101

Desloges, J. 1997 Les premières architectures funéraires de Basse-Normandie. In: C. Constantin, D. Mordant and D. Simonin, (eds) *La culture de Cerny. Nouvelle économie, nouvelle société au Néolithique*. Actes du Colloque international de Nemours, 9-10-11 mai 1994, Mémoires du Musée de Préhistoire d'Île-de-France, no. 6, 515-39

Dubouloz, J. 1994 Sur le vase dit «Grossgartach» de Passy-sur-Yonne: épilogue pour une attribution culturelle. *Bulletin de la Société Préhistorique Française* 91 (6), 385-93

Dubouloz, J. 2003 Datation absolue du premier Néolithique du Bassin Parisien: complément et relecture des données RRBP et VSG, *Bulletin de la Société Préhistorique Française* 100, 671-89.

Ducrocq, T. 1999 Le Mésolithique de la Vallée de la Somme (Nord de la France). In: A. Thévenin (ed) *L'Europe des Derniers Chasseurs. Epipaléolithique et Mésolithique*, Actes du 5e Colloque International UISPP, Commission XII, Grenoble, 18-23 septembre 1995, Éditions du CTHS, Paris, 247-61

Ducrocq, T. and Ketterer, I. 1995 Le Gisement Mésolithique du «Petit Marais», La Chaussée-Tirancourt (Somme), *Bulletin de la Société Préhistorique Française* 92 (2), 249-59

Duday, H. and Courtaud, P. 1998 La nécropole mésolithique de La Vergne (Charente-Maritime). In: J. Guilaine (ed) *Sépultures d'Occident et genèses des mégalithismes (9000–3500 avant notre ère)*, Éditions Errance, Paris, 25-37

Duhamel, P. 1997 (avec la collaboration de M. Fonton et H. Carré) La nécropole monumentale de Passy (Yonne): description d'ensemble et problèmes d'interprétation. In: C. Constantin, D. Mordant and D. Simonin (eds) *La culture de Cerny. Nouvelle économie, nouvelle société au Néolithique*. Actes du Colloque international de Nemours, 9-10-11 mai 1994, Mémoires du Musée de Préhistoire d'Île-de-France 6, 397-448

Duhamel, P. and Midgley, M.S. *forthcoming* Espaces, monumentalisme et pratiques funéraires des sociétés néolithiques en voie de hiérarchisation: les nécropoles monumentales Cerny du bassin Seine-Yonne, Actes du Colloque international, Musée des Tumulus de Bougon '*Origine et développement du mégalithisme de l'ouest de l'Europe*' du 26 au 30 octobre 2002, Bougon

Duhamel, P. and Mordant, D. 1997 Les nécropoles monumentales Cerny du bassin Seine-Yonne. In: C. Constantin, D. Mordant and D. Simonin (eds) *La culture de Cerny. Nouvelle économie, nouvelle société au Néolithique*. Actes du Colloque international de Nemours, 9-10-11 mai 1994, Mémoires du Musée de Préhistoire d'Île-de-France 6, 397-447.

Duhamel, P. and Prestreau, M. 1987 Les populations Néolithiques du Bassin Parisien, *Archéologia – Préhistoire et archéologie*, vol. 230 (décembre 1987), 54-65

Ebbesen, K. 1982 Yngre stenalders depotfund som bebyggelseshistorisk kildemateriale. In: H. Thrane (ed) *Om Yngre Stenalders Bebyggelseshistorie*, (Skrifter fra Historisk Institut No. 30), Odense Universitet, Odense, 60-79

Ebbesen, K. 1986 Megalithic Graves in Schleswig-Holstein, *Acta Archaeologica* 55, 117-42

Farruggia, J.-P., Guichard, Y. and Hachem, L. 1996 Les ensembles funéraires rubanés de Menneville, «Derrière le Village» (Aisne). In: P. Duhamel (ed) *La Bourgogne entre les Bassins Rhénan, Rhodanien et Parisien: Carrefour ou Frontière?*, Actes du XVIIIe Colloque interrégional sur le Néolithique Dijon, 25-27 octobre 1991 (Revue Archéologique de l'Est, Quatorzième supplément), Dijon, 119-74.

Farruggia, J.-P. 2002 Une crise majeure de la civilisation du Néolithique Danubien des années 5100 avant notre ère, *Archeologické rozhledy* 54, 44-98 (Festschrift for Marie Zápotocká).

Farruggia, J.-P., Kuper, R., Lüning, J. and Stheli, P. 1973 Der bandkeramische Siedlungsplatz Langweiler 2, Gemeinde Aldenhoven, Kreis Düren. *Rheinische Ausgrabungen* 13, Bonn

Fischer, A. 1982 Trade in Danubian shaft-hole axes and the introduction of Neolithic economy in Denmark, *Journal of Danish Archaeology* 1, 7-12

Fischer, A. 1985 Den vestsjællandske Åmose som kultur- og naturhistorisk reservat, *Fortidsminder, Antikvariske Studier* 7, 170-76

Florek, M. and Libera, J. 1997 Sprawozdanie z pierwszego sezonu badań na cmentarzysku kultury pucharów lejkowatych w Malicach Kościelnych, woj. Tarnobrzeskie, *Archeologia Polski Środkowowschodniej* 2, 24-30

Gabałówna, L. 1966 *Ze studiów nad grupą Brzesko-Kujawską Kultury Lendzielskiej. Brześć Kujawski Stanowisko 4*, Łódzkie Towarzystwo Naukowe, Łódź

Gabałówna, L. 1970 Wyniki analizy C-14 węgli drzewnych z cmentarzyska kultury pucharów lejkowatych na stanowisku 1 w Sarnowie – z grobowca 8 i niektóre problemy z nimi związane, *Prace i Materiały Muzeum Archeologicznego i Etnograficznego w Łodzi* 17, 77-91

Gerhards, G., Zariņa, G. and Zagorska, I. 2003 Burial traditions in the East Baltic Mesolithic. In: L. Larsson, H. Kindgren, K. Knutsson, D. Loeffler and A. Åkerlund (eds) *Mesolithic on the Move. Papers Presented at the Sixth International Conference on the Mesolithic in Europe, Stockholm 2000*, Oxbow Books, Oxford, 558-62

Glob, P.V. 1939 Der Einfluss der bandkeramischen Kultur in Dänemark, *Acta Archaeologica* 10, 131-40

Gramsch, B. 1973 *Das Mesolithikum im Flachland zwischen Elbe und Oder*, Deutscher Verlag der Wissenschaften, Berlin

Gramsch, B. 1993 Ein mesolithischer Birkenrindenbehälter von Friesack, *Veröffentlichungen des Brandenburgischen Landesmuseums für Ur- und Frühgeschichte* 27, 7-15

Grooth, M.E.Th.De 1991 Socio-economic aspects of Neolithic flint mining: a preliminary study, *Helinium* 31 (2), 153-89

Grygiel, R. 1986 The household cluster as a fundamental social unit of the Brześć Kujawski group of the Lengyel Culture in the Polish Lowlands, *Prace i Materiały Muzeum Archeologicznego i Etnograficznego w Łodzi* 31, 43-270

Gumiński, W. 1998 The Peat-bog Site Dudka, Masurian Lakeland: An Example of Conservative Economy. In: M. Zvelebil, L. Domańska, and R. Dennell, (ed) *Harvesting the Sea, Farming the Forest: The Emergence of Neolithic Societies in the Baltic Region*, Sheffield Academic Press, Sheffield, 103-9

Gumiński, W. and Fiedorczuk, J. 1990 Dudka 1: A Stone Age Peat-bog Site in Northeastern Poland, *Acta Archaeologica* 60 (1989), 51-70

Hamon, T., Irribarria, R., Rialland, Y. and Verjux, C. 1997 Le groupe de Chambon à la lumiere des découvertes récentes en région Centre. In: C. Constantin, D. Mordant and D. Simonin, (eds) *La culture de Cerny. Nouvelle économie, nouvelle société au Néolithique*. Actes du Colloque International de Nemours, 9-11 mai 1994. Nemours, Association pour la Promotion de la Recherche Archéologique en Île-de-France (Mémoires du Musée de Préhistoire d'Île-de-France 6), 195-217

Hartz, S. 1998 Frühbäuerliche Küstenbesiedlung im westlichen Teil der Oldenburger Grabenniederung (Wangels LA 505). Ein Vorbericht, *Offa* 54/55 (1997/98), 19-41

Hartz, S., Heinrich D. and Lübke H. 2000 Frühe Bauern an der Küste. Neue 14 C-Daten und aktuelle Aspekte zum Neolithisierungprozeß im norddeutschen Ostseeküstengebiet, *Praehistorische Zeitschrift* 75, 129-52

Hartz, S., Heinrich, D. and Lübke, H. 2002 Coastal Farmers – the neolithisation of northernmost Germany. In: A. Fischer and K. Kristiansen (eds) *The Neolithisation of Denmark. 150 years of debate*, J.R. Collis Publications, Sheffield, 321-40

Heinrich, D. 1998 Die Tierknochen des frühneolithischen Wohnplatzes Wangels LA 505. Ein Vorbericht, *Offa* 54/55 (1997/98), 43-48

Hodder, I. 1982 Theoretical archaeology: A reactionary view. In: I. Hodder (ed) *Symbolic and Structural Archaeology*, Cambridge University Press, Cambridge, 1-16

Hodder, I. 1984 Burials, houses, women and men in the European Neolithic. In: D. Miller and C. Tilley (eds) *Ideology, Power and Prehistory*, Cambridge University Press, Cambridge, 51-68

Hodder, I. 1990 *The Domestication of Europe. Structure and Contingency in Neolithic Societies*, Basil Blackwell, Oxford

Hoika, J. 1990 Megalithic Graves in the Funnel Beaker Culture of Schleswig-Holstein, *Przegląd Archeologiczny* 37, 53-119

Holsten, R. and Zahnow, G. 1920 Die steinzeitlichen Gräber des Kreises Pyritz, *Mannus* 11/12, 104-34

Ilett, M., Constantin, C., Coudart, A., Demoule J.-P. 1982 The late Bandkeramik of the Aisne valley: environment and spatial organisation, *Analecta Praehistorica Leidensia* 15, 45-61

Ilett, M. and Plateaux, M. 1995 *Le site néolithique de Berry-au-Bac «Le Chemin de la Pêcherie» (Aisne)*, CNRS Éditions, Paris

Ilkiewicz, J. 1989 From studies on cultures of the 4th millennium BC in the Central Part of the Polish Coastal area, *Przegląd Archeologiczny* 36, 17-55

Jacobs, K. 1995 Returning to Oleni'ostrov: Social, Economic, and Skeletal Dimensions of a Boreal Forest Mesolithic Cemetery, *Journal of Anthropological Archaeology* 14, 359-403

Jankowska, D. 1999 Megalithik und kujawische Gräber. In: K.W. Beinhauer, G. Cooney, C.E. Guksch and S. Kus (eds) *Studien zur Megalithik*, Beier and Beran, Weissbach, 215-26

Jażdżewski, K. 1936 *Kultura Pucharów Lejkowatych w Polsce Zachodniej i Środkowej*, Polskie Towarzystwo Prehistoryczne, Poznań.

Jażdżewski, K. 1938 Cmentarzyska kultury ceramiki wstęgowej i związane z nimi ślady osadnictwa w Brześćiu Kujawskim, *Wiadomości Archeologiczne* 15, 1-105

Jażdżewski, K. 1973 The Relations between Kujavian Barrows in Poland and Megalithic Tombs in northern Germany, Denmark and Western European Countries. In: G. Daniel and P. Kjærum (eds) *Megalithic Graves and Ritual*, Papers presented at the III Atlantic Colloquium, Moesgård 1969, Jutland Archaeological Society, Publications XI, København, 63-74

Jażdżewski, K. 1981 *Pradzieje Europy Środkowej*, Zakład Narodowy im. Ossolińskich, Wrocław

Jennbert, K. 1984 *Den produktiva gåvan. Tradition och innovation i Sydskandinavien för omkring 5300 år sedan*, Acta Archaeologica Lundensia 4:16, CWK Gleerup, Lund

Jennbert, K. 1998 'From the Inside': A Contribution to the Debate about the Introduction of Agriculture in southern Scandinavia. In: M. Zvelebil, R. Dennell and L. Domańska (eds) *Harvesting the Sea, Farming the Forest: The Emergence of Neolithic Societies in the Baltic Region*, Sheffield Academic Press, Sheffield, 31-5

Jeunesse, C. 1987 La Céramique de La Hoguette. Un nouvel 'élément non rubané' du Néolithique ancien de l'Europe du nord-ouest, *Cahiers alsaciens d'Archéologie, d'Art et d'Histoire* 30, 5-33

Jeunesse, C. 1995 Le vase de Passy et la synchronisation des séquences Néolithique moyen du Rhin et du Bassin Parisien – Problèmes de chronologie absolue, *Bulletin de la Société Préhistorique Française* 92 (1), 22-3

Jeunesse, C. 1996a Les groupes régionaux occidentaux du Rubané (Rhin et Bassin Parisien) à travers les pratiques funéraires, *Gallia Préhistoire* 37, 115-54

Jeunesse, C. 1996b Variabilité des pratiques funéraires et différenciation sociale dans le Néolithique ancien danubien, *Gallia Préhistoire* 38, 249-86

Jeunesse, C. 1997 *Pratiques Funéraires au Néolithique Ancien. Sépultures et nécropoles des sociétés danubiennes (5500–4900 av. J.-C.)*, Éditions Errance, Paris

Jeunesse, C. 1998 La néolithisation de l'Europe occidentale (VIIe – Ve millénaires av. J.-C.): nouvelles perspectives. In: *Les Derniers Chasseurs-Cueilleurs du Massif Jurassien et de ses Marges (13000–5500 avant Jésus-Christ)*, Centre Jurassien du Patrimoine, Lons-le-Saunier, 208-18

Jeunesse, C. 1999 La synchronisation des séquences culturelles des bassins du Rhin, de la Meuse et de la Seine et la chronologie du Bassin Parisien au Néolithique ancien et moyen (5200-4500 av. J.-C.) *Bulletin de la Société Préhistorique Luxembourgeoise* 20-21 (1998-99), 337-92

Jeunesse, C. 2000 Les composantes autochtone et danubienne en Europe centrale et occidentale entre 5500 et 4500 av. J.-C. : contacts, transferts, acculturations. In : *Les derniers chasseurs-cueilleurs d'Europe occidentale*, Actes du colloque international de Besançon, octobre 1998, Presses Universitaires Franc-Comtoises, Besançon, 361-78

Jeunesse, C. 2002 La coquille et la dent. Parure de coquillage et évolution des systèmes symboliques dans le Néolithique Danubien (5600-4500). In: J. Guilaine (ed) *Matériaux, Productions, Circulations du Néolithique à l'Âge du Bronze*, Éditions Errance, Paris, 49-64

Jeunesse, C., Nicod, P.-Y., van Berg, P.-L., Voruz, J.-L. 1991 Nouveaux témoins du Néolithique ancien entre Rhône et Rhin, *Annuaire de la Société suisse de Préhistoire et Archéologie* 74, 43-78.

Jørgensen, E. 1977 Brændende langdysser, *Skalk* 5, 7-13

Kalis, A. J. and Meurers-Balke, J. 1998 Die „Landnam" – Modelle von Iversen und Troels-Smith zur Neolithisierung des westlichen Ostseegebietes – ein Versuch ihrer Aktualisierung, *Praehistorische Zeitschrift* 73 (1), 1-24

Kannegaard Nielsen, E. and Brinch Petersen, E. 1993 Burials, people and dogs. In: S. Hvass and B. Storgaard (eds) *Digging into the Past. 25 Years of Archaeology in Denmark*, Aarhus Universitetsforlag, 76-81

Kayser, O. 1991 Le Mésolithique Breton: un état des connaissances en 1988. In: *Mésolithique et Néolithique en France et dans les Régions Limitrophes,* Actes du 113ᵉ Congrès National des Sociétés Savantes (Strasbourg, 5-9 avril 1988), Éditions du Comité des travaux historiques et scientifiques, Paris, 195-211

Keeley, L.H. and Cahen, D. 1989 Early Neolithic Forts and Villages in NE Belgium: A Preliminary Report, *Journal of Field Archaeology* 16, 157-76

Kjærum, P. 1969 Jættestuen Jordhøj, *Kuml* 1969, 9-66

Klassen, L. 1999 Prestigeøkser af sjældne alpine bjergarter: en glemt og overset fundgruppe fra ældre stenalderens slutning i Danmark, *Kuml* 1999, 11-51

Klassen, L. 2002 The Ertebølle culture and Neolithic continental Europe: traces of contact and interaction. In: A. Fischer and K. Kristiansen (eds) *The Neolithisation of Denmark. 150 years of debate*, J.R. Collis Publications, Sheffield, 305-17

Koch, E. 1998: *Neolithic Bog Pots from Zealand, Møn, Lolland and Falster*, Det Kongelige Nordiske Oldskriftselskab, København

Kozak-Zychman, W. and Gauda, E. 1998 Charakterystyka antropologiczna szczątków kostnych z grobów ludności kultury pucharów lejkowatych i kultury ceramiki sznurowej w Malicach Kościelnych (Stan. 1), woj. Tarnobrzeskie, *Archeologia Polski Środkowowschodniej* 3, 56-60

Krause, R. 1997 Un village rubané avec fossé d'enceinte et nécropole près de Vaihingen/Enz, Kr. Ludwigsburg. In: C. Jeunesse (ed) *Le Néolithique danubien et ses marges entre Rhin et Seine*, XXIIe colloque interrégional sur le Néolithique, Strasbourg 27-29 octobre 1995, Cahiers de l'Association pour la Promotion de la Recherche Archéologique en Alsace, Supplément 3, Strasbourg, 45-56

Kristensen, I.K. 1991 Storgård IV. An Early Neolithic Long Barrow near Fjelsø, North Jutland, *Journal of Danish Archaeology* 8 (1989), 72-87

Kruk, J. 1980 *Gospodarka w Polsce Południowo-Wschodniej w V-III Tysiącleciu p.n.e.*, Polska Akademia Nauk, Ossolineum, Wrocław

Kuper, L., Löhr, H., Lüning, J., Stehli, P. and Zimmermann, A. 1977 Der band-keramische Siedlungsplatz Langweiler 9, Gemeinde Aldenhoven, Kreis Düren. *Rheinische Ausgrabungen* 18, Bonn

Laporte, L. and Joussaume, R. 2002 Monuments funéraires Néolithiques dans l'Ouest de la France, Actes du Colloque international, Musée des Tumulus de Bougon '*Origine et développement du mégalithisme de l'ouest de l'Europe*' du 26 au 30 octobre 2002, Bougon, Résumés des communications, 48-56

Laporte, L., Joussaume, R. and Scarre, C. 2002 The perception of space and geometry. Megalithic monuments of west-central France in their relationship to the landscape. In: C. Scarre (ed) *Monuments and Landscape in Atlantic Europe. Perception and Society during the Neolithic and Early Bronze Age*, Routledge, London, 73-83

Larsson, L. 1988a A construction for Ceremonial Activities from the late Mesolithic, *Meddelanden från Lunds universitets historiska museum* 1987-1988, 5-18

Larsson, L. (ed) 1988b *The Skateholm Project. I. Man and Environment*, Almqvist and Wiksell International (Societatis Humaniorum Litterarum Lundensis LXXIX), Lund

Larsson, L. 1989a Big Dog and Poor Man: Mortuary Practices in Mesolithic Societies in Southern Sweden. In: T.B. Larsson and H. Lundmark (eds) *Approaches to Swedish Prehistory*, BAR Inter. Series 500, Oxford, 211-23

Larsson, L. 1989b Late Mesolithic Settlements and Cemeteries at Skateholm, southern Sweden. In: C. Bonsall (ed) *The Mesolithic in Europe*. Papers Presented at the Third International Symposium Edinburgh 1985, John Donald Publishers Ltd, Edinburgh, 367-78

Larsson, L. 1990 Dogs in Fraction – Symbols in Action. In: P.M. Vermeersch and P. van Peer (eds) *Contributions to the Mesolithic in Europe*. Papers Presented at the Fourth International Symposium 'The Mesolithic in Europe', Leuven 1990, Leuven University Press (Studia Praehistorica Belgica vol. 5), Leuven, 153-60

Larsson, L. 1995 Man and sea in southern Scandinavia during the late Mesolithic. The role of cemeteries in the view of society. In: A. Fischer (ed) *Man and Sea in the Mesolithic. Coastal settlement above and below present sea level, Proceedings of the International Symposium, Kalundborg, Denmark 1993*, Oxbow Books (Oxbow Monograph 53), Oxford, 95-104

Larsson, L. 1999 The Mesolithic period in southern Scandinavia: with special reference to burials and cemeteries, Paper presented at Mesolithic Scotland: The Early Holocene Prehistory of Scotland and its European Context, Conference in Edinburgh 5-7 November 1999

Lech, J. 1987 A Danubian raw material exchange network: a case study from Bylany. In: J. Rulf (ed) *Bylany Seminar 1987*, Archaeological Institute, Prague, 111-20

Le Roux, C.-T. (ed) 1992 *Paysans et Bâtisseurs. L'Émergence du Néolithique Atlantique et les Origines du Mégalithisme*, Actes du 17ᵉ Colloque interrégional sur le Néolithique, Vannes, 28-31 octobre 1990, Revue Archéologique de l'Ouest, Supplément 5

Le Roux, C.-T. 1999 *L'Outillage de Pierre polie en metadolerite du type A. Les ateliers de Plussulien (Côtes-d'Armor): Production et diffusion au Néolithique dans la France de l'ouest et au delà*, Travaux du Laboratoire «Anthropologie, Préhistoire et Quaternaire Armoricains», Unité mixte de Recherche 6566 «Civilisations atlantiques et Archéosciences», Université de Rennes I, Rennes

Lichardus, J. 1991 Die Kupferzeit als historische Epoche. Versuch einer Deutung. In: J. Lichardus (ed) *Die Kupferzeit als historische Epoche*, Symposium Saarbrücken und Otzenhausen 6.–13.11.1988, Rudolf Habelt GmbH, Bonn, 763-800

Lichardus, J. 1992 Passy et Cerny vus par la chronologie rhénane, *Saarbrücker Studien und Materialien zur Altertumskunde*, Sastuma 1, 9-16

Lichardus-Itten, M., Lichardus, J., Bailloud, G. and Cauvin, J. 1985 *La Protohistoire de l'Europe. Le Néolithique et le Chalcolithique entre le Méditerranée et la Mer Baltique*, Presses Universitaires de France, Paris

Liversage, D. 1981 Neolithic monuments at Lindebjerg, north-west Zealand, *Acta Archaeologica* 51 (1980), 85-152

Liversage, D. 1992 Barkær. Long Barrows and Settlements, Arkæologiske Studier IX, Akademisk Forlag, Universitetsforlaget I København

Lomborg, E. 1962 Zur Frage der bandkeramischen Einflüsse in Skandinavien, *Acta Archaeologica* 13, 1-38

Louwe Kooijmans, L.P. 1998 Understanding the Mesolithic/Neolithic Frontier in the Lower Rhine Basin, 5300-4300 cal. BC. In: M. Edmonds and C. Richards (eds) *Understanding the Neolithic of North-Western Europe*, Cruithne Press, Glasgow, 407-27

Lubbock, J. 1870 *The Origin of Civilisation and the Primitive Condition of Man*, Longmans, Green, London

Lüning, J. 1988 Frühe Bauern in Mitteleuropa im 6. und 5. Jahrtausend v. Chr., *Jahrbuch des Römisch-Germanischen Zentralmuseum Mainz* 35 (1987), 27-93

Lüning, J., Kloos, U. and Albert, S. 1989 Westliche Nachbarn der bandkeramischen Kultur: La Hoguette und Limburg, *Germania* 67 (2), 355-421

Lüning, J. and Stehli, P. 1994 *Die Bandkeramik im Merzbachtal auf der Aldenhovener Platte*. Habelt, Bonn

Madsen, T. 1979 Earthen Long Barrows and Timber Structures: Aspects of the Early Neolithic Mortuary Practice in Denmark, *Proceedings of the Prehistoric Society* 45, 301-20

Malm, T. 1995 Excavating submerged Stone Age sites in Denmark – the Tybrind Vig example. In: A. Fischer (ed) *Man and Sea in the Mesolithic. Coastal settlement above and below present sea level*, Proceedings of the International Symposium,

Kalundborg, Denmark 1993, Oxbow Books (Oxbow Monograph 53), Oxford, 385–96

Marchand, G. 1999 *La Néolithisation de l'ouest de la France: Caractérisation des industries lithiques,* BAR Inter. Series 748, Oxford

Marchand, G. 2000 La Néolithisation de l'ouest de la France: aires culturelles et transferts techniques dans l'industrie lithique, *Bulletin de la Société Préhistorique Française* 97, 377–403

Marciniak, A. 2003 People and animals in the early Neolithic in Central Europe. New approach to animal bones assemblages from farming settlements. In: A. Legakis, S. Sfenthourakis, R. Polymeni, M. Thessalou-Legaki (eds) *The New Panorama of Animal Evolution*, Proceedings of the 18th International Congress of Zoology, Pensoft, Sofia-Moscow, 309–17

Marciniak, M. 1993 Mesolithic burial and dwelling structure from the Boreal period excavated at Mszano site 14, Toruń district, Poland: preliminary report, *Mesolithic Miscellany* 14 (1 and 2), 7–11

Masset, C. and Soulier, P. (eds) 1995 *Allées couvertes et autres monuments funéraires du Néolithique dans la France du Nord-Ouest*, Éditions Errance, Paris

Mazurié de Keroualin, K. 2003 *Genèse et diffusion de l'agriculture en Europe: Agriculteurs-Chasseurs-Pasteurs,* Éditions Errance, Paris

Meiklejohn, C., Brinch Petersen, E. and Alexandersen, V. 1998 The Later Mesolithic Population of Sjælland, Denmark, and the Neolithic Transition. In: M. Zvelebil, R. Dennell and L. Domańska (eds) *Harvesting the Sea, Farming the Forest*, Sheffield Academic Press, Sheffield, 203–12

Midgley, M.S. 1985 *The Origin and Function of the Earthen Long Barrows of Northern Europe*, BAR Inter. Series 259, Oxford

Midgley, M.S. 1992 *TRB Culture. The First Farmers of the North European Plain*, Edinburgh University Press, Edinburgh

Midgley, M.S. 1997a The Earthen Long Barrows of Northern Europe: A Vision of the Neolithic World, *COSMOS (The Journal of Traditional Cosmology Society)* 11, 117–23

Midgley, M.S. 1997b The Earthen Long Barrow Phenomenon of Northern Europe and its Relation to the Passy-type Monuments of France. In: C. Constantin, D. Mordant and D. Simonin (eds) *La Culture de Cerny. Nouvelle économie, nouvelle société au Néolithique,* Actes du Colloque International de Nemours 1994, Mémoires du Musée de Préhistoire d'Île-de-France 6, 679–85

Midgley, M.S. 2000 The earthen long barrow phenomenon in Europe: Creation of monumental cemeteries. In: I. Pavlů (ed) *In Memoriam Jan Rulf,* Památky archeologické - Supplementum 13*, Praha, 255–65

Midgley, M.S. 2002 Early Neolithic farming communities in Northern Europe: Reconsideration of the TRB culture, *Archeologické rozhledy* 54 (1), 208–222 (Festschrift for Marie Zápotocká)

Midgley, M.S. *forthcoming* The Megalithic Tombs on the North European Plain, Actes du Colloque international, Musée des Tumulus de Bougon '*Origine et développement du mégalithisme de l'ouest de l'Europe*' du 26 au 30 octobre 2002, Bougon

Milisauskas, S. 1986 *Early Neolithic Settlement and Society at Olszanica*, Memoirs of the Museum of Anthropology 19, University of Michigan, Ann Arbor

Modderman, P.J.R. 1970 *Linearbandkeramik aus Elsloo und Stein*, Analecta Praehistorica Leidensia 3, Leiden

Modderman, P.J.R. 1981 Éléments non rubanés du Néolithique ancien entre les vallées du Rhin inférieur et de la Seine. I. Céramique du Limbourg: Rhénanie-Westphalie, Pays-Bas, Hesbaye, *Helinium* 21, 140-60

Modderman, P.J.R. 1988 The Linear Pottery Culture: Diversity in Uniformity, *Berichten van de Rijksdienst voor het Oudheidkundig Bodemonderzoek* 38, 63-139

Mohen, J.-P. 2003 *Cultes et Rituels mégalithiques. Les sociétés néolithiques de l'Europe du nord*, La Maison des Roches, Paris

Montelius, O. 1905 Orienten och Europa, *Antiqvarisk Tidskrift för Sverige* 13, 1-252

Mordant, C. and Mordant, D. 1970 Le site néolithique des Gours-aux-Lions à Marolles-sur-Seine (Seine-et-Marne), *Bulletin de la Société Préhistorique Française* 67 (1), 345-70

Mordant, D. 1991 Le site des Réaudins à Balloy (Seine-et-Marne). Premiers résultats. In: *Actes du 15ᵉ Colloque Interrégional sur le Néolithique, Châlons-sur-Marne, les 22 et 23 octobre 1988*, Association Régionale pour la Protection et l'Étude du Patrimoine Préhistorique, 33-43

Mordant, D. 1997 Le complexe des Réaudins à Balloy: enceinte et nécropole monumentale. In: C. Constantin, D. Mordant, and D. Simonin, (eds) *La Culture de Cerny. Nouvelle économie, nouvelle société au Néolithique*, Actes du Colloque International de Nemours 1994, Mémoires du Musée de Préhistoire d'Île-de-France No. 6, 449-80

Mordant, D. 1998 Émergence d'une architecture funéraire monumentale. In: J. Guilaine (ed) *Sépultures d'Occident et genèses des mégalithismes (9000–3500 avant notre ère), Séminaire du Collège de France*, Éditions Errance, Paris, 71-88

Mordant, D. and Simonin, D. 1997 Sites d'habitats Cerny. In: Constantin, C., Mordant, D. and Simonin, D., (ed) *La Culture de Cerny. Nouvelle économie, nouvelle société au Néolithique*, Actes du Colloque International de Nemours 1994, Mémoires du Musée de Préhistoire d'Île-de-France, No. 6, 319-39

Müller, F., Duhamel, P., Augereau, A. and Depierre, G. 1997 Une nouvelle nécropole monumentale Cerny à Gron «Les Sablons» (Yonne). In: C. Jeunesse (ed) *Le Néolithique danubien et ses marges entre Rhin et Seine*, Actes du 22ᵉ colloque interrégional sur le Néolithique, Strasbourg 27-29 octobre 1995. Cahiers de l'Association pour la Promotion de la Recherche Archéologique en Alsace, Supplément 3, 103-33

Müller, J. 2001 *Soziochronologische Studien zum Jung- und Spätneolithikum im Mittelelbe-Saale-Gebiet (4100–2700 v. Chr.)*, Verlag Marie Leidorf GmbH, Rahden/Westf

Myrhøj, H.M. and Willemoes, A. 1997 Wreckage from the Early Stone Age. In: L. Pedersen, A. Fischer and B. Aaby (eds) *The Danish Storebælt since the Ice Age – man, sea and forest*, A/S Storebælt Fixed Link, Copenhagen, 157-66

Nielsen, F.O. and Nielsen, P.O. 1985 Middle and Late Neolithic houses at Limensgård, Bornholm, *Journal of Danish Archaeology* 4, 101-14

Nielsen, P.O. 1984 Flint axes and megaliths – the time and context of the early dolmens in Denmark. In: G. Burenhult (ed) *The Archaeology of Carrowmore*, Theses and Papers in North-European Archaeology 14, Stockholm, 376-86

Niesiołowska-Śreniowska, E. 1999 The early TRB 'ploughmarks' from Sarnowo in central Poland: a new interpretation, *Oxford Journal of Archaeology* 18 (1), 17-22

Nilsson, S. 1868 *The Primitive Inhabitants of Scandinavia*, Longmans, Green and Co., London

Nowak, M. 1999 Drugi etap neolityzacji ziem polskich w świetle danych archeologicznych i palinologicznych, *Polish Botanical Studies Guidebook Series* 23, 39-77

Nowak, M. 2001 The second phase of Neolithization in east-central Europe, *Antiquity* 75, 582-92

Orschiedt, J. 1997 Sépultures rubanées en habitat dans le Bade-Wurtemberg. Études archéologiques et anthropologiques. In: C. Jeunesse (ed) *Le Néolithique danubien et ses marges entre Rhin et Seine*, XXIIe colloque interrégional sur le Néolithique Strasbourg 27-29 octobre 1995, Cahiers de l'Association pour la Promotion de la Recherche Archéologique en Alsace, Supplément no. 3, Strasbourg, 57-63

Paret, O. 1948 *Das neue Bild der Vorgeschichte*, August Schröder Verlag, Stuttgart

Pautreau, J.-P. 1991 Trois sépultures en fosses du Néolithique moyen à Antran (Vienne). In: J. Despriée (ed), La Région Centre. Carrefour d'Influences?, Actes du 14ᵉ Colloque Interrégional sur le Néolithique, Blois 16-17-18 octobre 1987, Société Archéologique Scientifique et Littéraire du Vendômois, Argenton-sur-Creuse, 131-42

Pautreau, J.-P., Farago-Szekeres, B. and Mornais, P. 2003 La nécropole néolithique de la Jardelle à Dissay (Vienne), *L'Archéologue 64 (février – mars 2003)*, 47-9

Pavlů, I. 2000 *Life on a Neolithic site. Bylany – Situational Analysis of Artefacts*, Institute of Archaeology, Prague

Pavúk, J. 1972 Neolithisches Gräberfeld in Nitra, *Slovenská Archeológia* 20 (1), 5-106

Pavúk, J. 1981 *Umenie a život doby kamennej*, Tatran, Bratislava

Pedersen, L. 1995 7,000 years of fishing: stationary fishing structures in the Mesolithic and afterwards. In: A. Fischer (ed) *Man and Sea in the Mesolithic. Coastal settlement above and below present sea level,* Proceedings of the International Symposium, Kalundborg, Denmark 1993 (Oxbow Monograph 53) Oxford, 75-86

Pedersen, L. 1997 They put fences into the sea. In: L. Pedersen, A. Fischer. and B. Aaby (eds) *The Danish Storebælt since the Ice Age – man, sea and forest*, A/S Storebælt Fixed Link, Copenhagen, 124-43

Péquart, M. and S.-J. 1954 *Hoëdic. Deuxième Station-Nécropole du Mésolithique Côtier Armoricain*, De Sikkel, Anvers

Péquart, M. and S.-J., Boule, M. and Vallois, H. 1937 *Téviec. Station-Nécropole Mésolithique du Morbihan*, Masson et Cie, Paris

Pétrequin, P. and Jeunesse, C. (eds) 1995 *La Hache de Pierre. Carrières vosgiennes et échanges de lames polies pendant le Néolithique (5400-2100 av. J.-C.)*, Éditions Errance, Paris

Pétrequin, P., Cassen, S., Croutsch, C. and Weller, O. 1997 Haches alpines et haches carnacéennes dans l'Europe du Ve millénaire, *Notae Praehistoricae* 17, 135-50

Piggott, S. 1937 The Long Barrow in Brittany, *Antiquity* 11, 441-55

Pleinerová, I. 1971 Kultovní objekty z pozdní doby kamenné v Březne u Loun, *Památky archeologické* 71, 10-60.

Podborský, V. and kolektiv 2002 *Dvě pohřebiště Neolitického lidu s Lineární keramikou ve Vedrovicích na Moravě*, Ústav archeologie a muzeologie, Filozofická fakulta Masarykovy univerzity, Brno

Prestreau, M. 1992 Le site néolithique et protohistorique des Falaises de Prépoux à Villeneuve-la-Guyard (Yonne), *Gallia Préhistoire* 34, 171-207

Price, N. 2001 (ed) *The Archaeology of Shamanism*, Routledge, London

Price, T.D. 2000 (ed) *Europe's First Farmers*, Cambridge University Press, Cambridge

Prodeo, F., Constantin, C., Martinez, R. and Toupet, C. 1997 La culture de Cerny dans la région Aisne-Oise. In: C. Constantin, D. Mordant and D. Simonin (eds) *La Culture de Cerny. Nouvelle économie, nouvelle société au Néolithique,* Actes du Colloque International de Nemours 1994, Mémoires du Musée de Préhistoire d'Île-de-France 6, 169-86

Raemaekers, D.C.M. 1999 *The Articulation of a 'New Neolithic'. The meaning of the Swifterbant Culture in the process of neolithisation in the western part of the North European Plain (4900–3400 BC),* Archaeological Studies Leiden University, Leiden

Rech, M. 1979 *Studien zu Depotfunden der Trichterbecher- und Einzelgrabkultur des Nordens,* (Offa-Bücher 39), Neumünster

Renfrew, C. 1972 Monuments, mobilization and social organization in neolithic Wessex. In: C. Renfrew (ed) *The explanation of culture change: models in prehistory*, Duckworth, London, 539-58

Renfrew, C. 1973 *Before Civilisation: The radiocarbon revolution and European Prehistory*, Jonathan Cape, London

Renfrew, C. 1976 Megaliths, territories and populations. In: S.J. de Laet (ed) *Acculturation and Continuity in Atlantic Europe*, De Tempel, Brugge, 198-220

Rudebeck, E. 1987 Flintmining in Sweden during the Neolithic period: new evidence from the Kvarnby-S. Sallerup area. In: G. de Sieveking and M.H. Newcomer (eds.), *The Human Uses of Flint and Chert*, Cambridge University Press, Cambridge, 151-57

Rulf, J. 1997 *Die Elbe-Provinz der Linearbandkeramik*, Památky archeologické – Supplementum 9, Archeologický ústav, Praha

Saxe, A. 1970 *Social Dimensions of Mortuary Practices*. Unpublished PhD Dissertation, University of Michigan

Scarre, C. 2002 Coast and Cosmos. The Neolithic monuments of northern Brittany. In: C. Scarre (ed) *Monuments and Landscape in Atlantic Europe. Perception and Society during the Neolithic and Early Bronze Age*, Routledge, London, 84-102

Schindler R. 1953 Die Entdeckung zweier jungsteinzeitlicher Wohnplätze unter dem Marschenschlick im Vorgelände der Boberger Dünen und ihre Bedeutung für die

Steinzeitforschung Nordwestdeutschlands, *Hammaburg* 4, 1–17

Schuldt, E. 1961 Abschliessende Ausgrabungen auf dem jungsteinzeitlichen Flachgräberfeld von Ostorf 1961, *Jahrbuch für Bodendenkmalpflege in Mecklenburg 1961*, 131–78

Schulting, R. and Richards, M. 2001 Dating Women and Becoming Farmers: New Palaeodietary and AMS Dating Evidence from the Breton Mesolithic Cemeteries of Téviec and Hoëdic, *Journal of Anthropological Archaeology* 20, 314–44

Schulting, R. 2003 The marrying kind: evidence for a patrilocal postmarital residence pattern in the Mesolithic of Southern Brittany? In: L. Larsson, H. Kindgren, K. Knutsson, D. Loeffler and A. Åkerlund (eds) *Mesolithic on the Move. Papers Presented at the Sixth International Conference on the Mesolithic in Europe, Stockholm 2000*, Oxbow Books, Oxford, 431–441

Schütz, C., Strien, H.-C., Taute, W. and Tillmann, W. 1992 Ausgrabungen in der Wilhelma von Stuttgart-Bad Cannstatt: die erste Siedlung der altneolithischen La Hoguette-Kultur, *Archäologische Ausgrabungen in Baden-Württemberg 1991*, 45–50

Schwabedissen, H. 1958 Die Ausgrabungen im Satruper Moor, *Offa*, vol. 16, 5–28.

Shanks, M. and Tilley, C. 1982 Ideology, Power and Ritual Communication: A Reinterpretation of Neolithic Mortuary Practices. In: I. Hodder (ed) *Symbolic and Structural Archaeology*, Cambridge University Press, Cambridge, 129–54

Sherratt, A. 1987 Wool, Wheels and Ploughmarks: Local Developments or Outside Introductions in Neolithic Europe? *Bulletin of the Institute of Archaeology (University of London)* 23, 1–15

Sherratt, A. 1990 The genesis of megaliths: monumentality, ethnicity and social complexity in Neolithic north-west Europe, *World Archaeology* 22(2), 147–67

Sherratt, A. 1991 Sacred and Profane Substances: the Ritual Use of Narcotics in Later Neolithic Europe. In: P. Garwood, D. Jennings, R. Skeates and J. Toms (eds) *Sacred and Profane*, Proceedings of a Conference on Archaeology, Ritual and Religion. Oxford 1989, Oxford University Committee for Archaeology, Monograph No.32, 50–64

Sherratt, A. 1995 Instruments of conversion: the role of megaliths in Mesolithic-Neolithic transition in north-west Europe, *Oxford Journal of Archaeology* 14(3), 245–60

Sidéra, I. 2000 Animaux domestiques, bêtes sauvages et objets en matières animales du Rubané au Michelsberg: De l'économie aux symboles, des techniques à la culture, *Gallia Préhistoire* 42, 107–94

Simonin, D., Bach, S., Richard, G. and Vintrou, J. 1997 Les sépultures sous dalle de type Malesherbes et la nécropole d'Orville. In: C. Constantin, D. Mordant and D. Simonin (eds) *La culture de Cerny. Nouvelle économie, nouvelle société au Néolithique*. Actes du Colloque international de Nemours, 9-10-11 mai 1994, Mémoires du Musée de Préhistoire d'Île-de-France, no. 6, 341–79

Skaarup, J. 1985a *Yngre Stenalder på øerne syd for Fyn*, Meddelelser fra Langelands Museum, Rudkøbing

Skaarup, J. 1985b *Stengade. Ein langeländischer Wohnplatz mit Hausresten aus der frühneolithischen Zeit*, Langelands Museum, Rudkøbing

Skaarup, J. 1995a Stone-Age Burials in Boats. In: O. Crumlin-Pedersen and B.M. Thye (eds) *The Ship as Symbol in Prehistoric and Mediaeval Scandinavia* (Studies in Archaeology and History 1), Nationalmuseet, København, 51-58

Skaarup, J. 1995b Hunting the hunters and fishers of the Mesolithic – twenty years of research on the sea floor south of Funen, Denmark. In: A. Fischer (ed) *Man and Sea in the Mesolithic. Coastal settlement above and below present sea level, Proceedings of the International Symposium, Kalundborg, Denmark 1993*, Oxbow Books (Oxbow Monograph 53), Oxford, 397-401

Šmíd, M. 2000 Drobné zjišť'ovací výzkumy na eneolitických mohylových pohřebištích střední Moravy. In: I. Pavlů (ed) *In Memoriam Jan Rulf,* Památky archeologické – Supplementum 13, Praha, 389-404

Šmíd , M. 2003 *Mohylová Pohřebiště Kultury Nálevkovitých Pohárů na Moravě,* Pravěk, Supplementum 11, Brno

Soudský, B. 1960 Station néolithique de Bylany, *Historica* 2, 5-36

Soudský, B. 1966 *Bylany, osada nejstarších zemědělců z mladší doby kamenné,* Československá akademie věd, Praha

Soudský, B. 1970 *Bylany. Analýza I* vols. 1-15 (manuscript), Praha

Spatz, H. 1997 La nécropole du Néolithique moyen (Hinkelstein, Grossgartach) de Trebur (Gross-Gerau, Hesse). In: C. Jeunesse (ed) *Le Néolithique danubien et ses marges entre Rhin et Seine,* actes du XXIIe colloque interrégional sur le Néolithique, Strasbourg 27-29 octobre 1995, Cahiers de l'Association pour la Promotion de la Recherche Archéologique en Alsace, Supplément no. 3, Strasbourg, 157-70

Sprockhoff, E. 1938 *Die nordische Megalithkultur,* Berlin

Stafford, M. 1999 *From Forager to Farmer in Flint: A Lithic Analysis of the Prehistoric Transition to Agriculture in Southern Scandinavia,* Aarhus University Press, Aarhus

Stäuble, H. 2002 From the air and on the ground: two aspects of the same archaeology? Round and linear ditch systems in North-Western Saxony, *Archeologické rozhledy* 54 (1), 301-313 (Festschrift for Marie Zápotocká)

Stehli, P. 1989 Merzbachtal – Umwelt und Geschichte einer bandkeramischen Siedlungskammer, *Germania* 67, 51-76

Strassburg, J. 1997 Inter the Mesolithic – Unearth Social Histories: Vexing Androcentric Sexing Through Strøby Egede, *Current Swedish Archaeology* 5, 155-78

Strassburg, J. 2000 *Shamanic Shadows. One Hundred Generations of Undead Subversion in Southern Scandinavia, 7000--4000 BC,* Stockholm Studies in Archaeology 20, Stockholm

Street, M., Jöris, O., Baales, M., Cziesla, E., Hartz, S., Heinen, M., Koch, I., Pada, C., Terberger, T. and Vollbrecht, J. 2003 Paléolithique Final et Mésolithique en Allemagne Reunifiée: Bilan Décennal. In: R. Desbrosse and A. Thévenin (eds) *Préhistoire de l'Europe. Des origines à l'Âge du Bronze,* Éditions du Comité des travaux historiques et scientifiques, Paris, 343-84

Taborin, Y. 1974 La parure en coquillage de l'Épipaléolithique au Bronze Ancien en France, *Gallia Préhistoire* 17, 101-79

Tainter, J.A. 1978 Mortuary practices and the study of prehistoric social systems, *Advances in Archaeological Method and Theory* 1, 105-41

Thévenin, A. 1999 Nouvelles considérations sur le Mésolithique du Nord-Est de la France. In: E. Cziesla, Th. Kersting and St. Pratsch (eds) *Den Bogen spannen... Festschrift für Bernhard Gramsch zum 65. Geburtstag*, Beiträge zur Ur- und Frühgeschichte Mitteleuropas 20, 235-45

Thrane, H. 1982 Dyrkningsspor fra yngre stenalder i Danmark. In: H. Thrane (ed) *Om Yngre Stenalders Bebyggelseshistorie*, Odense, 20-8

Tilley, C. 1994 *A Phenomenology of Landscape. Places, paths and monuments*, Berg, Oxford

Tilley, C. 1996 *An ethnography of the Neolithic. Early prehistoric societies in southern Scandinavia*, Cambridge University Press, Cambridge

Tilley, C. 1999 *The Dolmens and Passage Graves of Sweden. An Introduction and Guide*, Institute of Archaeology, University College London, London

Tresset, A. 1996 *Le rôle des relations homme/animal dans l'évolution économique et culturelle des sociétés des V^x-IV^x millénaires en Bassin Parisien, Approche ethno-zootechnique fondée sur les ossements animaux*, Thèse de Préhistoire-Ethnologie-Anthropologie, Université de Paris I Panthéon-Sorbonne

Trigger, B. 1990 Monumental architecture: a thermodynamic explanation of symbolic behaviour, *World Archaeology* 22(2), 119-32

Valais, A. 1995 Deux bâtiments atypiques associes à du matériel Cerny (Herblay, Val-d'Oise). In: *Actes du 20e colloque interrégional sur le Néolithique, Evreux 1993*, Revue Archéologique de l'Ouest, Supplément 7, 57-63

van Berg, P.-L. 1990 La Céramique du Limbourg et la Néolithisation de l'Europe occidentale. In :D. Cahen and M. Otte (eds) *Rubané et Cardial*, Actes du Colloque de Liège, novembre 1988, Études et Recherches Archéologiques de l'Université de Liège, Liège, 161-208

Vaquero Lastres, J. 1999 *Les extrêmes distincts. La configuration de l'espace dans les sociétés ayant bâti des tertres funéraires dans le Nord-Ouest ibérique*, BAR Inter. Series 821, Oxford

Veit, U. 1992 Burials within settlements of the Linienbandkeramik and Stichbandkeramik cultures of central Europe. On the social construction of death in early-Neolithic society, *Journal of European Archaeology* 1, 107-40

Velde, P. van de 1979 *On Bandkeramik social structure. An analysis of pot decoration and hut distributions from the Central European Neolithic communities of Elsloo and Hienheim*, Analecta Praehistorica Leidensia 12, Leiden

Verjux, C. 1999a Chronologie des rites funéraires mésolithiques à Auneau (Eure-et-Loir, France). In: A. Thévenin (ed) *L'Europe des Derniers Chasseurs. Epipaléolithique et Mésolithique*, Actes du 5e Colloque International UISPP, Commission XII, Grenoble, 18-23 septembre 1995, Éditions du CTHS, Paris, 293-302

Verjux, C. 1999b Des bâtiments circulaires du Néolithique moyen dans le Bassin parisien. In: *Camps, enceintes et structures d'habitats en France septentrionale, Résumés des communications, 24e Colloque interrégional sur le Néolithique*. Musée des Beaux-Arts d'Orléans, 19-21 novembre 1999, 34-5

Verjux, C. 2002 Une sepulture sous dalle originale à Auneau (Eure-et-Loir), Actes du Colloque international, Musée des Tumulus de Bougon '*Origine et développement du mégalithisme de l'ouest de l'Europe*' du 26 au 30 octobre 2002, Bougon, Résumés des communications, 130-31

Verjux, C. Dubois J.-P. and Tresset A. 1992 *Des derniers chasseurs aux premiers éleveurs-agriculteurs: 3000 ans d'occupations préhistoriques sur le site du «Parc du Château» à Auneau (Eure-et-Loir)*. Ed. Comité Archéologique d'Eure-et-Loir 1992

Weiner, J. 1997 A Bandkeramic Settlement with Wooden Well from Erkelenz-Kückhoven, Northrhine Westphalia (FRG). In: C. Jeunesse (ed) *Le Néolithique danubien et ses marges entre Rhin et Seine*, XXIIe colloque interrégional sur le Néolithique Strasbourg 27-29 octobre 1995, Cahiers de l'Association pour la Promotion de la Recherche Archéologique en Alsace, Supplément 3, Strasbourg, 401-5

Whittle, A. 1996 *Europe in the Neolithic. The Creation of New Worlds*, Cambridge University Press, Cambridge

Zápotocká, M. 1998a *Bestattungsritus des böhmischen Neolithikums (5500-4200 B.C.)*, Archeologický ústav AV ČR, Praha

Zápotocká, M. 1998b Die chronologische und geographische Gliederung der postlinearkeramischen Kulturgruppen mit Stichverzierung. In: J. Preuß (ed) *Das Neolithikum in Mitteleuropa: Kulturen – Wirtschaft – Umwelt vom 6. bis 3. Jahrtausend v. u. Z.*, Beier and Beran, Weissbach 286-306

Zich, B. 1993 Die Ausgrabungen chronisch gefährdeter Hügelgräber der Stein- und Bronzezeit in Flintbek, Kreis Rendsburg-Eckernförde. Ein Vorbericht, *Offa* 49/50 (1992/93), 15-31

Zvelebil, M. 1994 Plant Use in the Mesolithic and its Role in the Transition to Farming, *Proceedings of the Prehistoric Society* 60, 35-74

Zvelebil, M. and Rowley-Conwy, P. 1984 Transition to Farming in Northern Europe: A Hunter-Gatherer Perspective, *Norwegian Archaeological Review* 17, 104-28

Zvelebil, M. and Zvelebil, K. V. 1988 Agricultural transition and Indo-European dispersals, *Antiquity* 62, 574-83

INDEX

If you are interested in purchasing other books published by Tempus,
or in case you have difficulty finding any Tempus books in your local
bookshop,
you can also place orders directly through our website

www.tempus-publishing.com